table of contents

introduction

Why This Book?

It is important that we learn to engage in **conversation**, make meaning when **reading**, express ourselves through **writing**, and make a **presentation** to inform, educate, or entertain. These are pillars of literacy, which are essential for lifelong learning.

Literacy Mats delivers these pillars of literacy and core language arts academic standards in a way that takes the curriculum off the shelf and puts it in the hands of students, parents, and teachers as a shared learning tool. With Literacy Mats, we learn to learn.

Literacy Mats presents core literacy concepts and skills in four different ways: as a command, an enduring understanding, an essential question, and a learning point. At first, this seems redundant; but it's intentional. By thinking and reflecting about a concept or skill in different ways, we exercise our understanding in different ways.

Through Literacy Mats, we learn to apply the fundamentals of literacy. Prompts, questions, graphic organizers, and rubrics direct our learning and help us to develop critical reasoning and creative thinking through an inquiry-based approach. And, in the process, we are intentionally exposed to core language arts academic vocabulary.

Research shows that reading intelligence is the driving force in learning. Think about it. Queries such as "What do you think about the character's desires and struggles?" or "What do you think about the message of the story?" are most effective in getting us to think about what we read and to make meaning.

"What do you think?" These four simple words encourage us to read between the lines and to put two and two together. We learn to make meaning through inferences, interpretations, and reflections. As we develop our reading intelligence, we transition from learning to read to reading to learn.

With Literacy Mats, teachers and students and parents, as partners in learning, build a common language with shared understandings for the ABCs of literacy. Together, we grow.

I wrote this book in order to share with teachers, students, and parents everywhere what I have learned as a parent and educator about teaching purposeful reading, writing, and communication. In it, I lay out in simple terms the basics of how to learn to converse, read, write, and present. My aim is to take the mystery out of the process. It's really not hard.

How to Use This Book

Rather than make editions of Literacy Mats intended for each grade level per the traditional approach of educational publishers, I have written this book at an upper elementary reading level and it is intended to be used recursively (repeated application) year after year. As we grow and mature, the book's prompts, questions, graphic organizers, and rubrics take on a deeper meaning. A question such as "What do you think about the character's desires and struggles?" works with a simple chapter book at one reading level as well as with a classic novel at a higher reading level. Making meaning matches the level of reading. Through recursive application and learning with Literacy Mats, over time, the fundamentals of literacy gain depth and become a habit of mind.

I recommend introducing Literacy Mats as early as grade 3 and using this learning tool through grade 12. Students using Literacy Mats across grade levels for language arts, social studies, and science gain continuity of learning through the lens of literacy.

Teachers and students use Literacy Mats daily in the following ways:

> To plan units of study and lessons
> To develop foundational reading and writing skills through authentic fiction
> To develop foundational reading and writing skills through authentic nonfiction
> To develop conversation and presentation skills around authentic fiction and nonfiction
> At the start of a lesson to make explicit expectations for learning
> During instruction and modelling as an anchor chart
> During independent reading and writing as a guide
> At the end of the lesson as a formative assessment tool
> Anytime reading, writing, conversing, or presenting

Four Pillars of Literacy for Lifelong Learning

With Literacy Mats, we meet high expectations for achievement of core academic literacy standards. Through four pillars of literacy for lifelong learning, we learn to learn.

1. Conversation to build and shape understanding
2. Reading to make meaning
3. Writing to communicate and express meaning
4. Presentation to inform, educate, or entertain

I hope that this book helps you learn to become a conversationalist, reader, writer, and presenter, and I hope that everyone grows to be the self-directed lifelong learner they were born to be.

Brian Kissman, Author

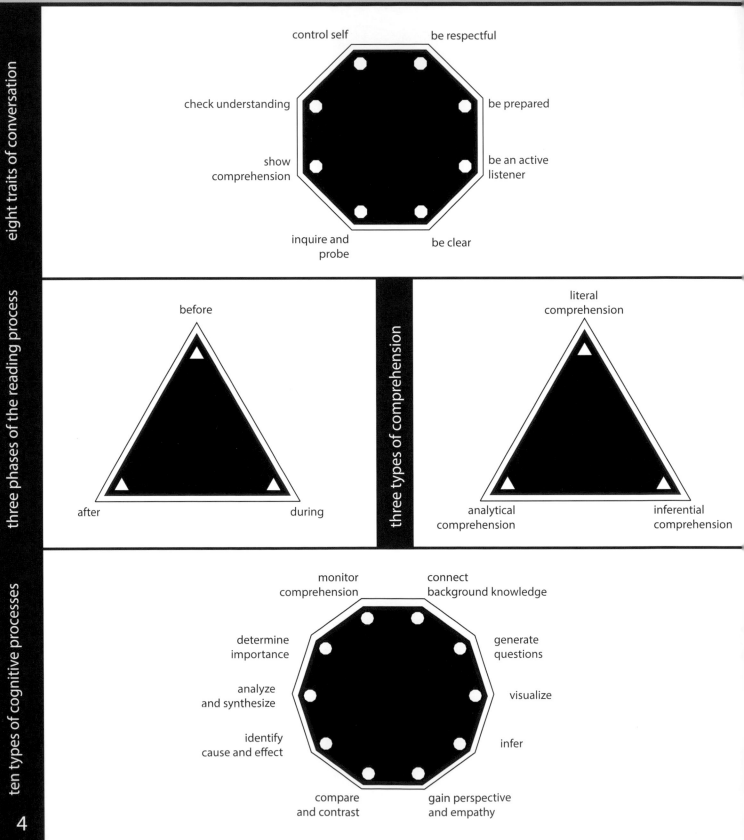

eight traits of conversation

- control self
- be respectful
- check understanding
- be prepared
- show comprehension
- be an active listener
- inquire and probe
- be clear

three phases of the reading process

- before
- after
- during

three types of comprehension

- literal comprehension
- analytical comprehension
- inferential comprehension

ten types of cognitive processes

- monitor comprehension
- connect background knowledge
- determine importance
- generate questions
- analyze and synthesize
- visualize
- identify cause and effect
- infer
- compare and contrast
- gain perspective and empathy

You know the 26 letters of the alphabet.
Here are the ABCs of literacy.

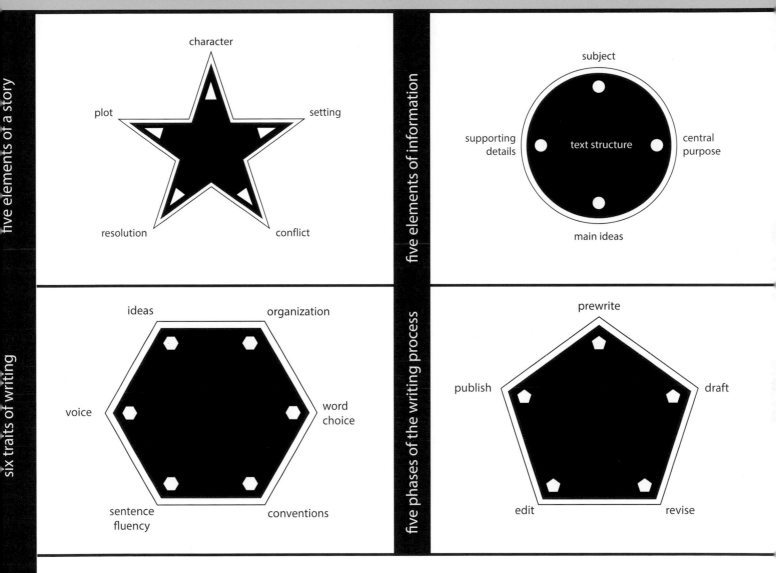

five elements of a story

character
setting
conflict
resolution
plot

five elements of information

subject
central purpose
main ideas
supporting details
text structure

six traits of writing

ideas
organization
word choice
conventions
sentence fluency
voice

five phases of the writing process

prewrite
draft
revise
edit
publish

four traits of presentation

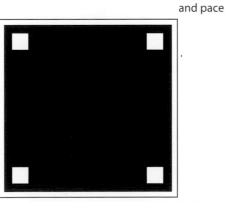

volume and clarity
fluency, expression, and pace
preparation and rehearsal
body language and eye contact

Pillars
of Literacy

Conversation

traits of
conversation

eight traits of conversation

traits of conversation

We engage in conversation as learners, as professionals, and in social settings.

We build, shape, and grow our knowledge, understandings, and experiences through conversation. As lifelong learners, conversation provides us the opportunity to exercise thinking, creativity, and problem solving.

The ability to effectively engage in conversation is developed through a knowledge and skill set. The Eight Traits of Conversation represents that knowledge and skill set.

traits
of conversation
eight traits of conversation

traits of conversation

1. **Be Respectful**
   Appreciate others' thinking. Encourage others to participate in the conversation. Take the conversation seriously. Disagree politely.

2. **Be Prepared**
   Focus on the topic, activate background knowledge, and make connections. Prepare for conversations about shared reading by generating questions, making notes, and marking passages. Participate and contribute to the conversation.

3. **Be An Active Listener**
   Look at the person speaking. Ask questions based upon what others have said. Build upon and add to what others have to say.

4. **Be Clear**
   Speak clearly so that others understand. Speak in complete sentences. Express thoughts precisely and with details. Support thinking with evidence.

5. **Inquire and Probe**
   Ask multiple, open-ended questions. Investigate, examine, scrutinize, and analyze others' thoughts and ideas.

6. **Show Comprehension**
   Exercise cognitive processes, meta-cognition, and comprehension through the elements of literature in order to demonstrate understanding.

7. **Check Understanding**
   Examine thinking. Listen to the inner conversation. Reflect upon and communicate how thoughts have changed. Share with others when understanding breaks down.

8. **Control Self**
   Take turns and give others the opportunity to speak. Monitor contributions to the conversation in terms of how often and how much. Listen without interrupting. Use wait time. Pay attention to volume and tone.

traits
of conversation
eight traits of conversation

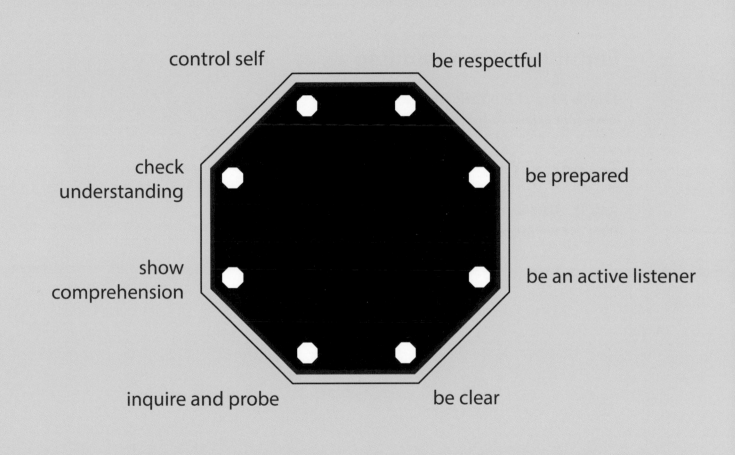

control self

be respectful

check
understanding

be prepared

show
comprehension

be an active listener

inquire and probe

be clear

1. Be Respectful

Appreciate others' thinking. Encourage others to participate in the conversation. Take the conversation seriously. Disagree politely.

Enduring Understanding

Think About It. Talk About It.
Respect cultivates integrity.

Essential Question

Ask It. Answer It.
Why are we respectful?

Learning Point
1. Conversationalists show respect. They value others' ideas.
   They are polite, thoughtful, caring, and interested in what others have to say.
   When they disagree, they do so respectfully. They engage everyone in the discussion.

traits of conversation

eight traits of conversation

2. Be Prepared

Focus on the topic, activate background knowledge, and make connections. Prepare for conversations about shared reading by generating questions, making notes, and marking passages. Participate and contribute to the conversation.

Enduring Understanding

Think About It. Talk About It.
Preparation enables participation.

Essential Question

Ask It. Answer It.
Why do we prepare?

Learning Point
1. Conversationalists prepare to contribute to a discussion by focusing on the topic, activating background knowledge, and making connections. In doing so, they are ready to engage in conversation with a sense of purpose.

3. Be an Active Listener

Look at the person speaking. Ask questions based upon what others have said. Build upon and add to what others have to say.

Enduring Understanding

Think About It. Talk About It.
Active listening affirms thoughts and ideas.

Essential Question

Ask It. Answer It.
Why do we actively listen?

Learning Point
1. Conversationalists look at the person speaking and respond directly to what they have to say either by asking questions or building upon ideas.

4. Be Clear

Speak clearly so that others understand.
Speak in complete sentences. Express thoughts precisely and with details. Support thinking with evidence.

Enduring Understanding

Think About It. Talk About It.
Clarity strengthens communication.

Essential Question

Ask It. Answer It.
Why do we communicate with clarity?

Learning Point
1. Conversationalists speak with clarity so that others are able to understand their ideas and thinking. They express their thoughts with complete sentences and in detail, using precise and accurate words. They support their thinking with evidence.

5. Inquire and Probe

Ask multiple, open-ended questions. Investigate, examine, scrutinize, and analyze others' thoughts and ideas.

Enduring Understanding

Think About It. Talk About It.
When we inquire and probe, we gain insight.

Essential Question

Ask It. Answer It.
Why do we inquire and probe?

Learning Point
1. Conversationalists inquire and probe beyond what might seem evident to investigate, examine, scrutinize, and analyze others' thoughts and ideas. They seek clarity and a deeper understanding.

6. Show Comprehension

Exercise cognitive processes, meta-cognition, and comprehension to demonstrate understanding.

Enduring Understanding

Think About It. Talk About It.
Showing comprehension builds conversation.

Essential Question

Ask It. Answer It.
Why do we show comprehension?

Learning Point
1. Conversationalists exercise cognitive processes, meta-cognition, and comprehension to build and shape understanding.
2. Conversationalists summarize, make inferences and interpretations, and reflect upon the gist to build and shape understanding.

7. Check Understanding

Examine thinking. Listen to the inner conversation.
Reflect upon and communicate how thoughts have changed.
Share with others when understanding breaks down.

Enduring Understanding

Think About It. Talk About It.
Checking understanding confirms or suspends assumptions.

Essential Question

Ask It. Answer It.
Why do we check understanding?

Learning Point
1. Conversationalists share with others when their understanding breaks down, make it known when their thoughts have changed, and inquire to confirm or suspend assumptions.

8. Control Self

Take turns and give others the opportunity to speak.
Monitor contributions to the conversation in terms of how often
we speak and how much we say when we speak. Listen without
interrupting. Use wait time. Pay attention to volume and tone.

Enduring Understanding

Think About It. Talk About It.
Controlling self demonstrates composure.

Essential Question

Ask It. Answer It.
Why do we control self?

Learning Point
1. Conversationalists demonstrate self-control in terms of how often they speak
   and how much they say when they speak. They do not interrupt others.
   Conversationalists use wait time to assure that everyone participates in the
   conversation. They are mindful of their volume and tone.

Conversation Prompts

Question Prompts

Why...?

How...?

What do you think...?

The signal words "Why," "How," and "What do you think" lead to thick questions. Question prompts lead to insights, interpretations, and reflections.

Probe Prompts

Why do you say that?

Why do you think that?

What makes you think that?

Can you explain why you think that?

Would you please explain that further?

Would you provide some evidence for that idea?

What facts do you recall to support your thinking?

Probe prompts show the speaker that there is active listening taking place. When the listener inquires and probes beyond the initial question and response, the conversation is extended, becomes strong, and brings clarity and deeper understanding.

Response Prompts

Because...

For instance...

For example...

Let me explain...

The author said...

On page _____ , it said...

From the reading we know that..

I agree..

To piggyback on...   To add on...

Evidence-based response prompts guide conversationalists to stay on topic longer.

Tentative Response Prompts

Maybe...

Probably...

It could be...

It might be that...

Perhaps...

I would suggest...

I'm not sure, but I wonder if...

More important than "right answers," tentative response prompts lead to open, respectful risk taking and sharing. We can't exercise critical reasoning and creative thinking if we are shy about being unsure or hesitant to share our thoughts.

Pillars of Literacy

Reading

phases of the reading process

three phases of the reading process

reading process

The Reading Process is a three-step process, which becomes a habit of mind and strengthens our ability to make meaning when we read:

1. BEFORE
    Think about what is already known or experienced in connection to what is about to be read.

2. DURING
    Read and think to make meaning.

3. AFTER
    Make time to converse and write about what has been read to build and shape understanding.

The Reading Process enables us to readily engage in reading because it carries forward meaning and gives us purpose. As a routine, it gives us structure and direction.

phases of
the reading process
three phases of the reading process

reading process

Before. During. After. Think of the colors of a traffic light. Red. Yellow. Green.

1. **Before**
   Think about what is already known or experienced in connection to what is about to be read.

   Before we read the light is RED. We stop and think about our background knowledge and personal experiences in connection to what is about to be read.

   Discuss what is already known about the themes, topics, and ideas of the story or information. Talk about background knowledge and personal experiences relative to a theme or topic. This brings forward prior knowledge and understanding, and prepares us to make meaning as we read.

2. **During**
   Read and think to make meaning.

   During reading the light is YELLOW. We go slow, reading and thinking to make meaning.

   Read, pause to think, make notes, and mark important passages of interest in the book with stickies. Make it a habit of mind to read, think, and make meaning.

3. **After**
   Make time to converse and write about what has been read to build and shape understanding.

   After reading the light is GREEN. We go, engaging in conversation or writing about what has been read to make meaning.

   Partner with a reading buddy or come together with a group to discuss the reading. Reference tracks of thinking and be prepared to support interpretations and reflections with evidence from the text and background knowledge. Write in a journal to build and shape understanding.

phases of the reading process
three phases of the reading process

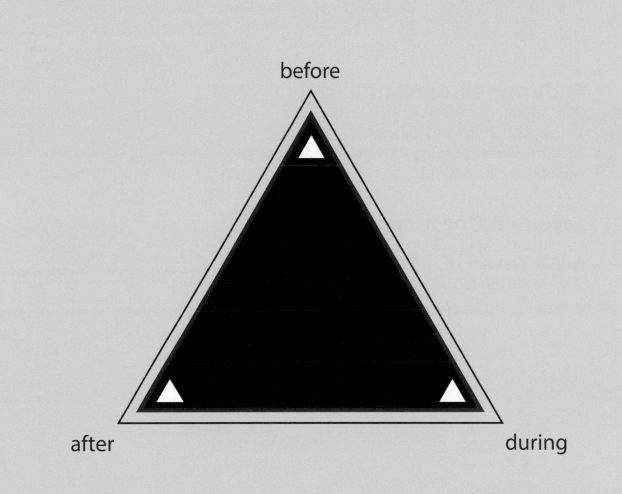

phases of
the reading process
three phases of the reading process

1. Before

Think about what is already known or experienced in connection to what is about to be read.

Enduring Understanding

Think About It. Talk About It.
Thinking before reading activates background knowledge and makes connections.

Essential Question

Ask It. Answer It.
Why do we think before we read?

Learning Point
1. Readers think about what they know and have experienced in relation to a text's theme, subject, and ideas prior to reading to prepare to make meaning.

phases of
the reading process
three phases of the reading process

2. During

Read and think to make meaning.

Enduring Understanding

Think About It. Talk About It.
Reading and thinking carries forward meaning.

Essential Question

Ask It. Answer It.
Why do we think as we read?

Learning Point
1. Readers pause and think as they read to make meaning.
2. Readers exercise cognitive processes, meta-cognition, and comprehension as they read.

3. After

Make time to converse and write about what has been read to build and shape understanding.

Enduring Understanding

Think About It. Talk About It.
Conversing and writing after reading builds and shapes understanding.

Essential Question

Ask It. Answer It.
Why do we converse or write after we read?

Learning Point
1. Readers engage in conversation and writing about what they have read to build and shape understanding. They summarize, interpret, and reflect.

Reading intelligence is the driving force in learning.

Pillars
of Literacy

Reading

types of comprehension

three types of comprehension

types of comprehension

When we read, whether it is a story or information, we learn to think. We make meaning and comprehend in three ways:

One, we make meaning through literal comprehension. We demonstrate understanding by retelling and summarizing in our own words what has been made explicit.

Two, we make meaning through inferential comprehension. We demonstrate understanding by making inferences, interpretations, and reflections about what is implicit in the text. We do this based upon evidence from the text and in connection to our background knowledge and personal experience.

Three, we make meaning by seeing through the eyes of a writer, analyzing and evaluating the text for traits of good writing. We refer to this as analytical comprehension.

types of comprehension

three types of comprehension

types of comprehension

1. **Literal Comprehension**
   Retell or summarize the facts to communicate what is made explicit through the elements of a story (fiction).

   Summarize the facts to communicate what is made explicit through the elements of information (nonfiction).

2. **Inferential Comprehension**
   Express what is implicit within the text. Make text-to-text, text-to-self, and text-to-world connections in order make inferences, interpretations, and reflections.

3. **Analytical Comprehension**
   Evaluate the quality of writing in a story or information against the Traits of Writing.

   Evaluate the quality of small moment scenes in narrative writing.

   Evaluate the quality of what we notice, think, and realize in non-narrative writing.

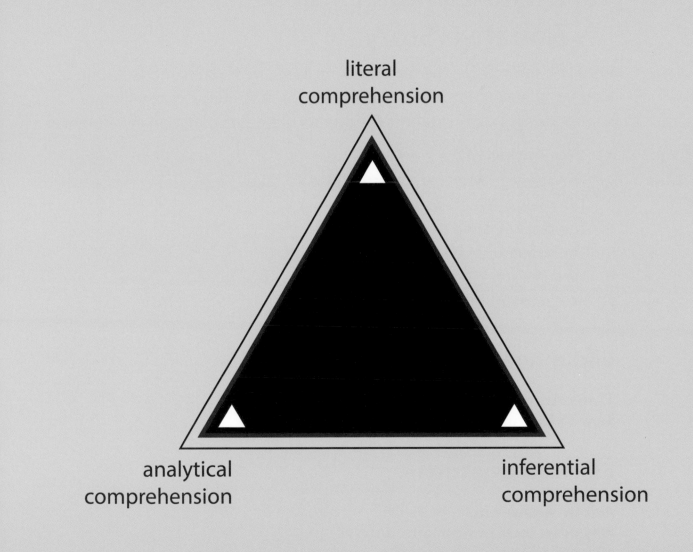

literal
comprehension

analytical
comprehension

inferential
comprehension

1a. Literal Comprehension: Narrative/Story

Retell or summarize the facts to communicate what is made explicit through the elements of a story (fiction). One strategy for retelling or summarizing a story presents the literary elements of fiction in sequence:

1. The message of the story
2. The setting - when and where the story takes place
3. The main character(s)
4. The story's conflict
5. The sequence of events
6. How the story's conflict is resolved
7. Restatement of the story's message

Enduring Understanding

Think About It. Talk About It.
Summarizing makes explicit a sequence of events.

Essential Question

Ask It. Answer It.
Why do we retell or summarize a story?

Learning Point
1. Readers retell or summarize, in their own words, what has been made explicit in a story (fiction) to demonstrate literal comprehension.
2. Readers retell or summarize by covering the elements of a story.

1b. Literal Comprehension: Non-narrative/Information

Summarize the facts to communicate what is made explicit through the elements of information (nonfiction). One formula for summarizing the literary elements of information presents the "Five Ws and an H" in sequence:

1. Who or what
2. What they did or what it did
3. Where it took place
4. When it took place
5. Why it happened
6. How it happened

Enduring Understanding

Think About It. Talk About It.
Summarizing makes explicit ideas and important details.

Essential Question

Ask It. Answer It.
Why do we summarize a piece of information text?

Learning Point
1. Readers retell or summarize, in their own words, what has been made explicit in an information text (nonfiction) to demonstrate literal comprehension.
2. Readers retell or summarize by covering the elements of information.

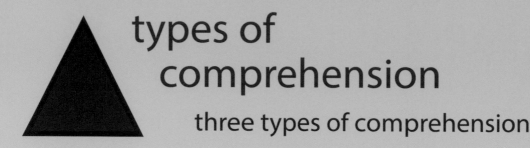

2. Inferential Comprehension

Express what is implicit within the text. Make text-to-text, text-to-self, and text-to-world connections to make inferences, interpretations, and reflections.

Enduring Understanding

Think About It. Talk About It.
Inferences supported by evidence imply meaning.

Essential Question

Ask It. Answer It.
Why do we make inferences?

Learning Point
1. Readers read between the lines and put two and two together to think about what is implied - what might be true.
2. Readers carry forward thinking and make connections to make inferences, interpretations, and reflections.

3. Analytical Comprehension

Evaluate the quality of writing in a story or information against the Traits of Writing.

Evaluate the quality of small moment scenes in narrative writing.

Evaluate the quality of expressing what we notice, think, and realize in non-narrative writing.

Enduring Understanding

Think About It. Talk About It.
Reading develops writing.

Essential Question

Ask It. Answer It.
Why do we analyze writing?

Learning Points
1. Readers analyze the quality of writing against the six Traits of Writing.
2. Readers analyze the quality of small moment scenes in narrative writing.
3. Readers analyze the quality of expressing what they notice, think, and realize in non-narrative writing.

Build and Shape Understanding through Conversation

Think about an illustration (any illustration). Then read a passage that supports the illustration. Engage in conversation with a reading partner to share your thinking.

First, what is your comprehension of the illustration?

How would you summarize what is made explicit by the illustration?

What might you infer is implied by the illustration?

types of comprehension

three types of comprehension

Max and Sam had just completed the first day at their new school. Heading out of the building together into the late afternoon sunlight, they were quite surprised to see some of their new friends surrounding another student they had met. The situation did not look comfortable. As they came closer, they could overhear what was going on.

"Hey Earl, I bet you got those hot shoes at that new store," mocked Brad, the group leader. "Do you know what I would do if I had a pair of shoes like that? I would be cooler than cool." The pack howled in laughter as they closed the circle. The timid boy, Earl, was trapped like a rabbit surrounded by wolves. When he tried to step away, the gang of boys blocked his path. Max started toward the group to break it up, but Sam snatched Max by the arm, pulling him back.

"Max, those guys are very popular in this school. They are part of the in-crowd. If you get into this now, we are going to be a part of the out-crowd," cautioned Sam. Max gave Sam a stern look. Sam knew what his look meant. Sam let go and walked alongside Max. They calmly slid in amongst the boys.

"Hey, Earl, we were looking for you. Come on. If we are going to make it to the game, we have to get going. Hey gentlemen, great meeting you earlier today. We'll catch up with you tomorrow," Max said as they calmly strolled away.

"Are you alright, Earl?" asked Sam.
"Yes. Thanks, guys," sighed Earl in relief.
"Max, you are the man!" Sam exclaimed. "I'm sorry for not being ready to do the right thing." Sam felt a bit ashamed.
"No worries. Thanks for being by my side, Sam," replied Max.

Second, what is your comprehension of the passage?

How would you summarize what is made explicit by the passage?

What might you infer is implied by the passage?

What is your analysis of the quality of this writing? What traits of writing stand out? How effectively does the writer zoom in and show a small moment scene? Or, if you are analyzing a non-narrative piece, how effectively does the author breathe life into the writing by expressing what we notice, think, and realize?

How might you revise the piece of writing to improve it?

Pillars
of Literacy

Reading

cognitive
processes

ten types of cognitive processes

cognitive processes

It is natural that we think as we read, but when we are able to name our thinking with a common language and shared understandings, we are empowered to become intentional about developing and exercising our thinking skills as a habit of mind.

There are ten types of cognitive processes that we refer to as the ABCs of critical reasoning. We use them to understand complex situations, generate solutions to problems, and nurture new insight.

These cognitive processes become even more powerful when we reflect upon how we have used them, aiming to self-evaluate and improve our cognitive processes. We refer to this as meta-cognition (thinking about thinking).

Meta-cognition involves three types of knowledge:
> knowledge of cognitive process
> knowledge of strategies and tasks
  (which cognitive process to apply to which problem or task)
> knowledge of self

cognitive
processes

ten types of cognitive processes

cognitive processes

1. **Connect Background Knowledge**
Make connections to what is being read with prior knowledge and personal experiences.

2. **Generate Questions**
Ask open-ended questions to propel reading forward. Ask why a character behaves or feels a certain way. Ask what are the implications of specific events or choices.

3. **Visualize**
Form mental sensory and emotional images to make meaning and deepen understanding. Read, think, and create movies in the mind.

4. **Infer**
Think about what is implied. Read between the lines and put two and two together. Make predictions and come to conclusions supported by evidence.

5. **Gain Perspective and Empathy**
See through the eyes of the character (perspective) and feel the character's emotions (empathy). Walk in the shoes of the character.

6. **Compare and Contrast**
Identify and think about similarities and differences between people, places, objects, and events – within the text and between the text and the real world.

7. **Identify Cause and Effect**
Determine why an event happened and the impact it has on a character or situation. Think, "because this happened, that happened."

8. **Analyze and Synthesize**
Understand by taking apart the constitution or structure of a person, place, object, or event (analyze). Understand by putting knowledge and ideas together to solve problems and create solutions (synthesize).

9. **Determine Importance**
Decide what ideas and details matter most to make meaning, to make decisions, and to solve problems.

10. **Monitor Comprehension**
Recognize when understanding breaks down. Ask questions and reread to make meaning and clarify understanding.

cognitive processes

ten types of cognitive processes

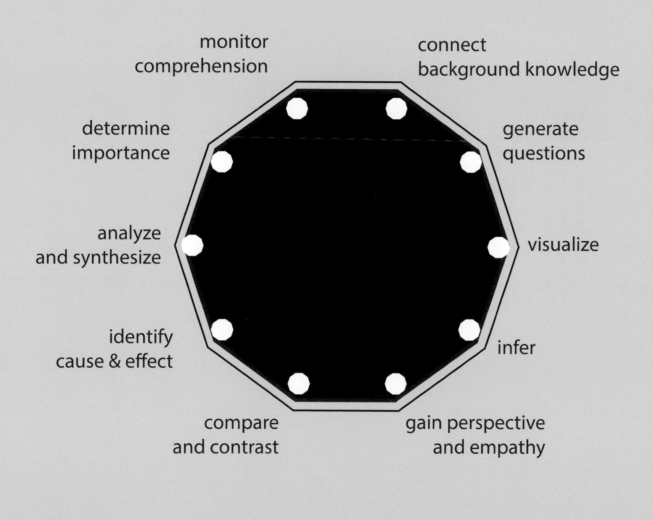

monitor comprehension

connect background knowledge

determine importance

generate questions

analyze and synthesize

visualize

identify cause & effect

infer

compare and contrast

gain perspective and empathy

1. Connect Background Knowledge

Make connections to what is being read with prior knowledge and personal experiences.

Enduring Understanding

Think About It. Talk About It.
Making connections grows perspective.

Essential Question

Ask It. Answer It.
Why do we make connections and activate background knowledge?

Learning Points
1. Readers make meaning by making connections between what they know, personal experiences, and the story or information they are reading.
2. Readers make connections in three ways: text-to-text, text-to-self, text-to-world.

2. Generate Questions

Ask open-ended questions to propel reading forward.
Ask why a character behaves or feels a certain way?
Ask what are the implications of specific events or choices?

Enduring Understanding

Think About It. Talk About It.
Generating questions stimulates thinking.

Essential Question

Ask It. Answer It.
Why do we generate questions?

Learning Point
1. Readers ask open-ended questions to make meaning.
   They wonder why a character behaves a certain way or why specific events happen?
   They use simple yet powerful words. They ask, "What do you think?" and
   "Why do you think that?"

3. Visualize

Form mental sensory and emotional images to make meaning.
Read, think, and create movies in the mind.

Enduring Understanding

Think About It. Talk About It.
Visualizing creates mental sensory and emotional images.

Essential Question

Ask It. Answer It.
Why do we visualize?

Learning Point
1. Readers visualize, seeing beyond the words.
2. Readers form sensory and emotional images to make meaning.

4. Infer

Think about what is implied. Read between the lines and put two and two together. Make predictions and come to conclusions supported by evidence.

Enduring Understanding

Think About It. Talk About It.
Inferences supported by evidence imply meaning.

Essential Question

Ask It. Answer It.
Why do we make inferences?

Learning Points
1. Readers think about what is implied and make inferences.
2. Readers make predictions and come to conclusions.
3. Readers bring together inferences to make interpretations and reflections.

5. Gain Perspective and Empathy

See through the eyes of the character (perspective) and feel the character's emotions (empathy). Walk in the shoes of the character.

Enduring Understanding

Think About It. Talk About It.
Perspective gains insight; empathy gains understanding.

Essential Question

Ask It. Answer It.
Why are perspective and empathy important?

Learning Points
1. Readers see through the eyes of the character (perspective) and feel the character's emotions (empathy) to make meaning.
2. Readers walk in the shoes of a character to know a character's desires and struggles.

6. Compare and Contrast

Identify and think about similarities and differences between people, places, objects, events, and ideas – within the text and between the text and the world.

Enduring Understanding

Think About It. Talk About It.
Compare and contrast of similarities and differences grows understanding.

Essential Question

Ask It. Answer It.
Why do we compare and contrast?

Learning Point
1. Readers compare and contrast similarities and differences between people, places, objects, events, and ideas to make meaning.
2. Readers grow understanding when they compare and contrast.

7. Identify Cause and Effect

Determine why an event happened and the impact it has on a character or situation.   Think, "because this happened, that happened."

Enduring Understanding

Think About It. Talk About It.
Cause and effect relationships show consequence.

Essential Question

Ask It. Answer It.
Why do think about cause and effect relationships?

Learning Point
1. Readers think about cause and effect relationships to make meaning about a character's actions or choices, or about a specific event and the resulting consequences.

8. Analyze and Synthesize

Understand by taking apart the constitution or structure of a person, place, object, or event (analyze).

Understand by putting knowledge and ideas together to solve problems and create solutions (synthesize).

Enduring Understanding

Think About It. Talk About It.
Analysis breaks down meaning.

Synthesis produces new meaning and innovation.

Essential Question

Ask It. Answer It.
Why do we analyze?

Why do we synthesize?

Learning Points
1. Readers analyze a person, place, object, or event to make meaning by thinking about the parts.
2. Readers synthesize ideas, events, and new knowledge with existing knowledge to make meaning, solve problems, and create solutions.

9. Determine Importance

Decide what ideas and details matter most to make meaning, solve problems, and make decisions.

Enduring Understanding

Think About It. Talk About It.
Determining importance depends upon purpose.

Essential Question

Ask It. Answer It.
Why do we determine importance?

Learning Point
1. Readers determine importance by identifying ideas and details that matter most depending upon purpose.

10. Monitor Comprehension

Recognize when understanding breaks down.
Ask questions and reread to make meaning and clarify misunderstandings.

Enduring Understanding

Think About It. Talk About It.
Monitoring comprehension confirms meaning.

Essential Question

Ask It. Answer It.
Why do we monitor comprehension?

Learning Point
1. Readers know when understanding breaks down and react by asking questions or rereading to make meaning and clarify understanding.
2. Readers monitor the inner conversation.

Pillars
of Literacy

Reading

★ star points

five elements of a story

elements of a story

When we read a story (fiction), we enter a new world. We meet characters, learn about times and places, become aware of challenges and conflicts, and see those challenges and conflicts being overcome. Each story is different, and each imaginary world is unique.

But each story also has shared elements, no matter when or where it occurs. There is a main character and secondary characters. There is a setting and sometimes multiple settings. There is a central conflict, and that conflict is most often resolved, which is the resolution. And, there is a plot, the sequence of events through which the story is told – the story mountain.

Every story has these elements in common. When we learn to think about the story through its elements, we are able to make meaning.

character

a person, imaginary being, or animal in a story;
within a story there are main characters, and
there may be secondary characters

setting

the time, place, and surroundings
in which the story occurs —
including the past, present, and future

conflict

a problem or disagreement in a story,
which typically is resolved; within a story
there is a main conflict, and there may be
secondary conflicts

resolution

the solving of, or solution to, the main conflict in
a story; within a story the resolution is typically
determined toward the end; the resolution
brings a natural, thought-provoking, or surprise
ending to the story

plot

a connected series of events in a story;
within a story there is a main plot, and there
may be subplots; a plot line has five parts

> exposition
introduction of the characters, setting, and background information
> rising action
the dialogue and action that present an unfolding conflict
> climax
the high point or turning point of action in the story
> falling action
the dialogue and action that lead to the story's resolution
> resolution
the solution to the conflict and a satisfying end to the story

star
points

five elements of a story

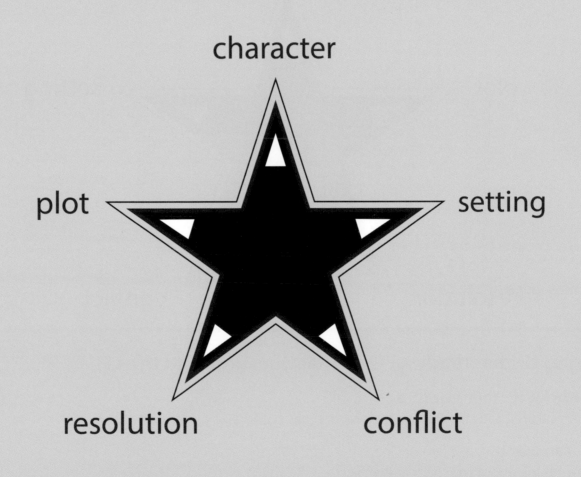

character

plot

setting

resolution

conflict

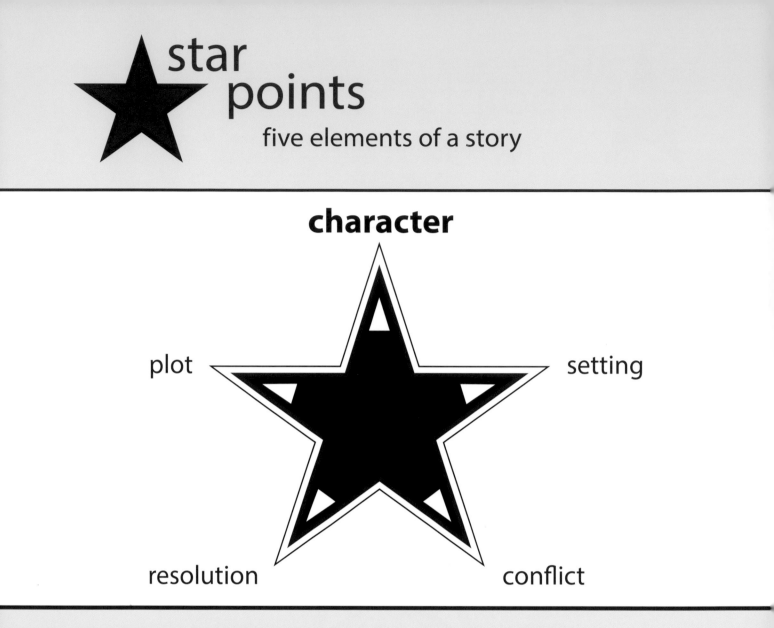

★ star
points

five elements of a story

character

plot

setting

resolution

conflict

Enduring Understanding, Essential Question, and the LP

Think About It. Talk About It.
Characters' desires and struggles reveal the author's purpose and message.

Ask It. Answer It.
Why do we think about the main characters?

Learning Points
1. Readers think about the character's desires and struggles.
2. Readers walk in the shoes of the character, entering the imaginary world of the story.
3. Readers come to know characters by their actions, choices, relationships, and by the objects that are important to them. And, they notice when a character is acting out of character.
4. Readers examine ways others interact with the main character, and they notice patterns of behavior.
5. Readers think about how the secondary characters in a story have meaningful roles, through which they learn about the main character.
6. Readers determine a character's personality traits and anticipate the character's response to events.
7. Readers think about how characters change across the events of the story.
8. Readers differentiate between a static character (no change over the course of the story) and a dynamic character (changes over the course of the story).

character

definition >

a person, imaginary being, or animal in a story;
within a story there are main characters, and
there may be secondary characters

questions for meaningful conversation

questions >

1. Who wants what? What are the character's desires?
2. How does the character struggle as a result of her/his desires?
3. What are the personality traits of the character?
4. How does the character view herself/himself?
5. How do others view the character?
6. What do you think about the character's choices?
7. How does the character's personality traits affect her/his choices?
8. What is important to the character? Why?
9. What relationships and objects are important to the character? Why?
10. What do you think about the relationships between characters?
11. What is learned about the main characters through secondary characters?
12. Why did the character act this way?
13. Was it right or wrong for the character to act this way? Why?
14. What did the character get from acting this way?
15. How am I like or unlike the character?
16. How does the character's desires and struggles reveal the author's message?
17. How does the setting put the story in context?
18. How does the setting impact the character and contribute to the mood of the story?
19. How would you describe the type of conflict(s) within the story?
    - > person against person
    - > person against self
    - > person against nature
    - > person against time
    - > person against society
    - > person against fate
20. How does the conflict develop?
21. What actions or events lead to the conflict's resolution?
22. How does the resolution bring a natural, thought-provoking, and/or surprise ending to the story.
23. What enduring understandings or essential questions arise from this story?
24. What are the big themes or lessons learned within this story? What's the gist?
25. How have the lessons learned changed the way I think?

prompts >

literal

Who…
What…
Why…
Where…
When…
How…
Name and define…
List…
Give the reasons why…
Provide support for…

inferential

What do you think…
Why do you think…
I wonder…
What if…
Predict and substantiate…
What do you do when…
What can be exciting about…
What would you do if…
What is your opinion about…
How does this connect with…

analytical

How effectively does the author show, not tell small moment scenes:
Setting?   Action?   Thoughts and Feelings?   Dialogue?

What do you think about the quality of the Traits of Writing:
Ideas?   Organization?   Voice?
Word Choice?   Sentence Fluency?   Conventions?

★ star points

five elements of a story

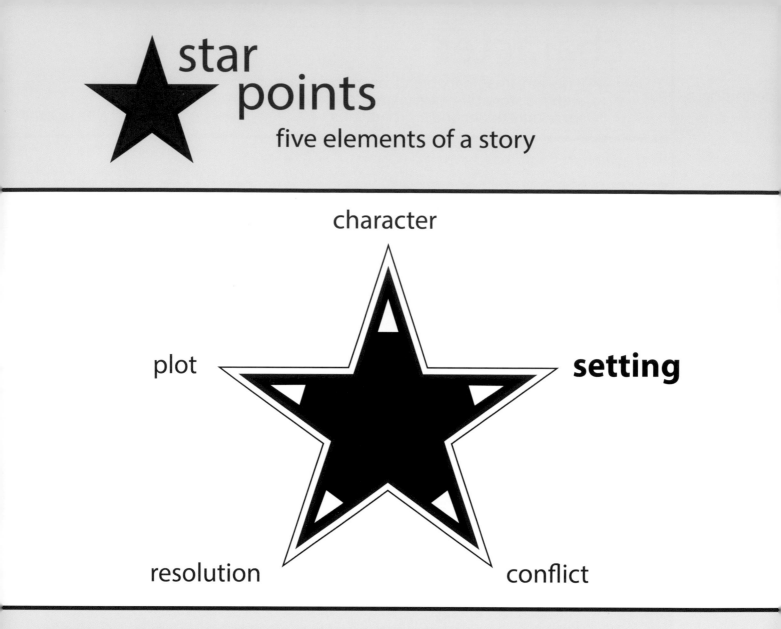

character

plot

setting

resolution

conflict

Enduring Understanding, Essential Question, and the LP

Think About It. Talk About It.
The setting reflects context and mood.

Ask It. Answer It.
Why do we think about the setting?

Learning Points
1. Readers recognize how the setting (time and place, including the past, present, and future) puts the story in context.
2. Readers interpret how the setting affects the character.
3. Readers reflect upon how the setting contributes to the mood of the story.

setting

the time, place, and surroundings in which the story occurs including the past, present, and future

questions for meaningful conversation

1. Who wants what? What are the character's desires?
2. How does the character struggle as a result of her/his desires?
3. What are the personality traits of the character?
4. How does the character view herself/himself?
5. How do others view the character?
6. What do you think about the character's choices?
7. How does the character's personality traits affect her/his choices?
8. What is important to the character? Why?
9. What relationships and objects are important to the character? Why?
10. What do you think about the relationships between characters?
11. What is learned about the main characters through secondary characters?
12. Why did the character act this way?
13. Was it right or wrong for the character to act this way? Why?
14. What did the character get from acting this way?
15. How am I like or unlike the character?
16. How does the character's desires and struggles reveal the author's message?
17. **How does the setting put the story in context?**
18. **How does the setting impact the character and contribute to the mood of the story?**
19. How would you describe the type of conflict(s) within the story?
    > person against person   > person against self
    > person against nature   > person against time
    > person against society   > person against fate
20. How does the conflict develop?
21. What actions or events lead to the conflict's resolution?
22. How does the resolution bring a natural, thought-provoking, and/or surprise ending to the story.
23. What enduring understandings or essential questions arise from this story?
24. What are the themes or lessons learned within this story? What's the gist?
25. How have the lessons learned changed the way I think?

literal

Who…
What…
Why…
Where…
When…
How…
Name and define…
List…
Give the reasons why…
Provide support for…

inferential

What do you think…
Why do you think…
I wonder…
What if…
Predict and substantiate…
What do you do when…
What can be exciting about…
What would you do if…
What is your opinion about…
How does this connect with…

analytical

How effectively does the author show, not tell small moment scenes:
Setting?   Action?   Thoughts and Feelings?   Dialogue?

What do you think about the quality of the Traits of Writing:
Ideas?   Organization?   Voice?
Word Choice?   Sentence Fluency?   Conventions?

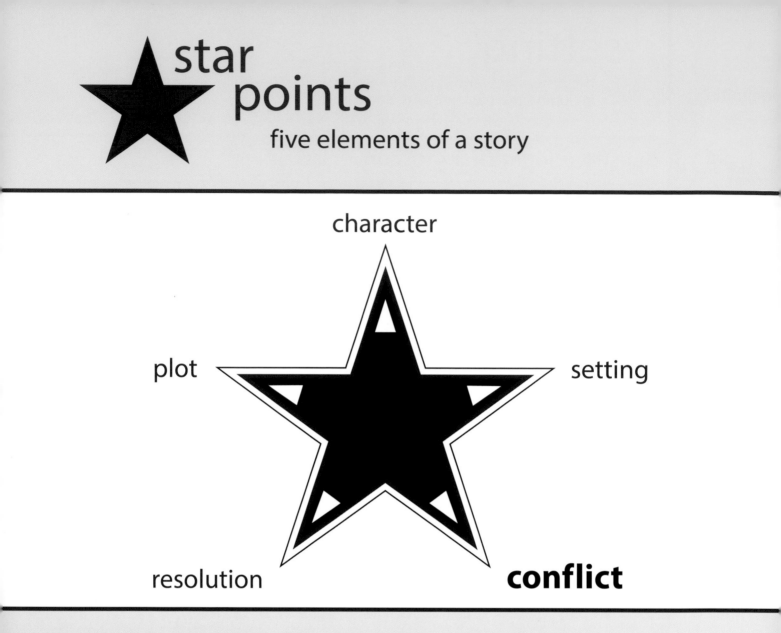

star points

five elements of a story

character

plot

setting

resolution

conflict

Enduring Understanding, Essential Question, and the LP

Think About It. Talk About It.
The conflict evolves through rising actions.

Ask It. Answer It.
Why do we think about the conflict?

Learning Points
1. Readers anticipate how the conflict of a story might unfold through the character's desires and struggles across the rising action.
2. Readers recognize how the conflict is made clear at the high point or a turning point in the story. This is the climax of the story.
3. Readers anticipate the climax is near when the character's desires and struggles seem to fully play out; when the suspense builds to a turning point.
4. Readers categorize the conflict of the story as being one or more of the following:
    > person against person   > person against self   > person against nature
    > person against time   > person against society   > person against fate

definition >

conflict

a problem or disagreement in a story, which typically is resolved; there is a main conflict, and there may be secondary conflicts

questions for meaningful conversation

questions >

1. Who wants what? What are the character's desires?
2. How does the character struggle as a result of her/his desires?
3. What are the personality traits of the character?
4. How does the character view herself/himself?
5. How do others view the character?
6. What do you think about the character's choices?
7. How does the character's personality traits affect her/his choices?
8. What is important to the character? Why?
9. What relationships and objects are important to the character? Why?
10. What do you think about the relationships between characters?
11. What is learned about the main characters through secondary characters?
12. Why did the character act this way?
13. Was it right or wrong for the character to act this way? Why?
14. What did the character get from acting this way?
15. How am I like or unlike the character?
16. How does the character's desires and struggles reveal the author's message?
17. How does the setting put the story in context?
18. How does the setting impact the character and contribute to the mood of the story?
19. **How would you describe the type of conflict(s) within the story?**
    - > **person against person**   > **person against self**
    - > **person against nature**   > **person against time**
    - > **person against society**   > **person against fate**
20. **How does the conflict develop?**
21. What actions or events lead to the conflict's resolution?
22. How does the resolution bring a natural, thought-provoking, and/or surprise ending to the story.
23. What enduring understandings or essential questions arise from this story?
24. What are the themes or lessons learned within this story? What's the gist?
25. How have the lessons learned changed the way I think?

prompts >

literal

Who…
What…
Why…
Where…
When…
How…
Name and define…
List…
Give the reasons why…
Provide support for…

inferential

What do you think…
Why do you think…
I wonder…
What if…
Predict and substantiate…
What do you do when…
What can be exciting about…
What would you do if…
What is your opinion about…
How does this connect with…

analytical

How effectively does the author show, not tell small moment scenes:
Setting?   Action?   Thoughts and Feelings?   Dialogue?

What do you think about the quality of the Traits of Writing:
Ideas?   Organization?   Voice?
Word Choice?   Sentence Fluency?   Conventions?

star points

five elements of a story

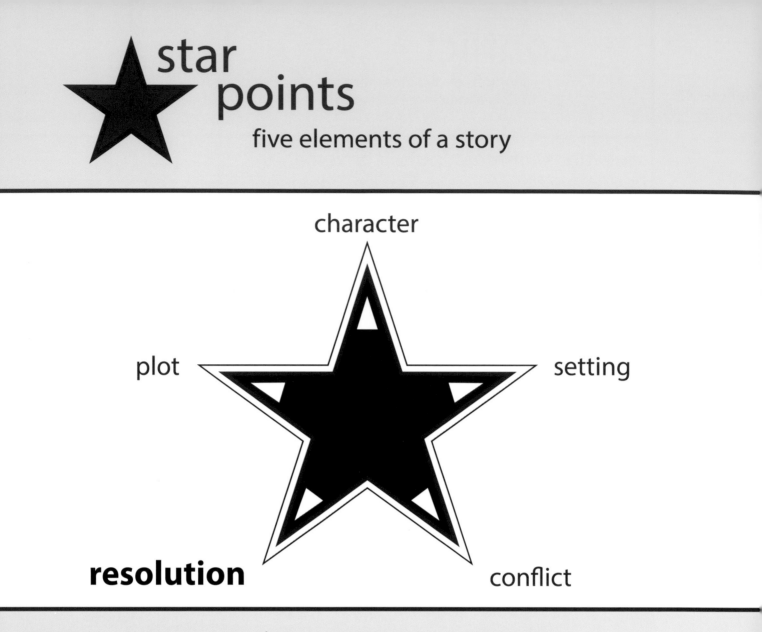

character

plot

setting

resolution

conflict

Enduring Understanding, Essential Question, and the LP

Think About It. Talk About It.
The resolution comes through falling actions.

Ask It. Answer It.
Why do we think about the resolution?

Learning Points
1. Readers know that the falling action of the story leads to the resolution.
2. Readers reflect upon the story, thinking about how the resolution to the conflict brings a natural, thought-provoking, and/or surprise ending to the story.
3. Readers recognize that the resolution to the conflict reflects what the characters have learned about life through the events of the story.

resolution

the solving of, or solution to, the main conflict in a story; within a story the resolution is typically determined toward the end; the resolution brings a natural, thought-provoking, and/or surprise ending to the story

questions for meaningful conversation

1. Who wants what? What are the character's desires?
2. How does the character struggle as a result of her/his desires?
3. What are the personality traits of the character?
4. How does the character view herself/himself?
5. How do others view the character?
6. What do you think about the character's choices?
7. How does the character's personality traits affect her/his choices?
8. What is important to the character? Why?
9. What relationships and objects are important to the character? Why?
10. What do you think about the relationships between characters?
11. What is learned about the main characters through secondary characters?
12. Why did the character act this way?
13. Was it right or wrong for the character to act this way? Why?
14. What did the character get from acting this way?
15. How am I like or unlike the character?
16. How does the character's desires and struggles reveal the author's message?
17. How does the setting put the story in context?
18. How does the setting impact the character and contribute to the mood of the story?
19. How would you describe the type of conflict(s) within the story?
    > person against person
    > person against nature
    > person against society
    > person against self
    > person against time
    > person against fate
20. How does the conflict develop?
21. **What actions or events lead to the conflict's resolution?**
22. **How does the resolution bring a natural, thought-provoking, and/or surprise ending to the story.**
23. What enduring understandings or essential questions arise from this story?
24. What are the themes or lessons learned within this story? What's the gist?
25. How have the lessons learned changed the way I think?

literal

Who…
What…
Why…
Where…
When…
How…
Name and define…
List…
Give the reasons why…
Provide support for…

inferential

What do you think…
Why do you think…
I wonder…
What if…
Predict and substantiate…
What do you do when…
What can be exciting about…
What would you do if…
What is your opinion about…
How does this connect with…

analytical

How effectively does the author show, not tell small moment scenes:
Setting?   Action?   Thoughts and Feelings?   Dialogue?

What do you think about the quality of the Traits of Writing:
Ideas?   Organization?   Voice?
Word Choice?   Sentence Fluency?   Conventions?

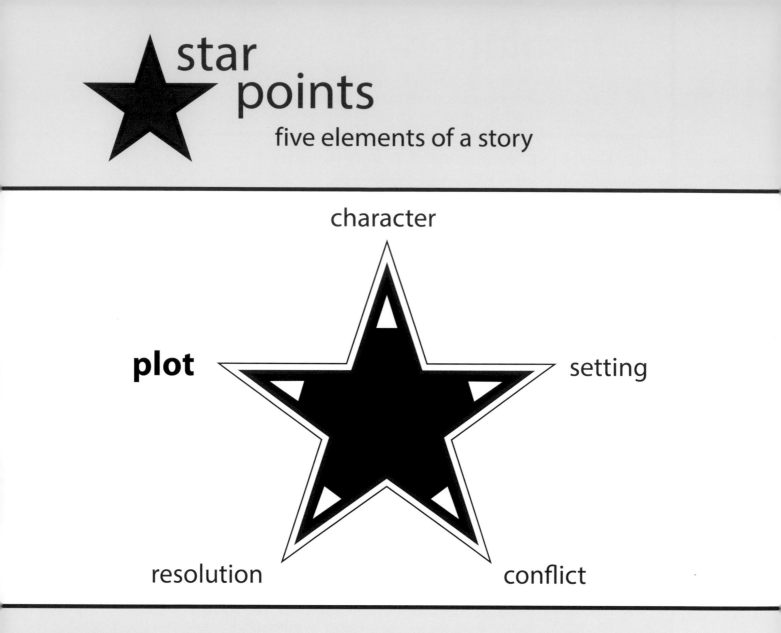

star points
five elements of a story

character

plot

setting

resolution

conflict

Enduring Understanding, Essential Question, and the LP

Think About It. Talk About It.
The plot provides structure to a story.

Ask It. Answer It.
How does the exposition "set up" the story?
How do the rising actions unfold the character's desires and struggles?
How does the climax change the course of the story?
How do the falling actions lead to the resolution?
How does the plot deliver the message of the story?

Learning Points
1. Readers know and understand the plot (story mountain) and its five parts: Exposition, Rising Action, Climax, Falling Action, and Resolution.
2. Readers carry forward inferences across the story to make interpretations and reflections about the story, supported by evidence from the text.
3. Readers think about how a character's actions and choices across events of the story may be symbolic of the story's theme and message.
4. Readers think about stand understand the story's message, which reflects the author's purpose.
5. Readers develop enduring understandings and generate essential questions from the story's plot.

plot

a connected series of events in a story; within a story there is a main plot, and there may be subplots; a plot line has five parts:

definition >

> exposition: introduction of the characters, setting, and background information
> rising action: the dialogue and action that present an unfolding conflict
> climax: the high point or turning point of action in the story
> falling action: the dialogue and action that lead to the story's resolution
> resolution: the solution to the conflict and a satisfying end to the story

questions for meaningful conversation

questions >

1. Who wants what? What are the character's desires?
2. How does the character struggle as a result of her/his desires?
3. What are the personality traits of the character?
4. How does the character view herself/himself?
5. How do others view the character?
6. What do you think about the character's choices?
7. How does the character's personality traits affect her/his choices?
8. What is important to the character? Why?
9. What relationships and objects are important to the character? Why?
10. What do you think about the relationships between characters?
11. What is learned about the main characters through secondary characters?
12. Why did the character act this way?
13. Was it right or wrong for the character to act this way? Why?
14. What did the character get from acting this way?
15. How am I like or unlike the character?
16. How does the character's desires and struggles reveal the author's message?
17. How does the setting put the story in context?
18. How does the setting impact the character and contribute to the mood of the story?
19. How would you describe the type of conflict(s) within the story?
    > person against person   > person against self
    > person against nature   > person against time
    > person against society   > person against fate
20. How does the conflict develop?
21. What actions or events lead to the conflict's resolution?
22. How does the resolution bring a natural, thought-provoking, and/or surprise ending to the story.
23. **What enduring understandings or essential questions arise from this story?**
24. **What are the themes or lessons learned within this story? What's the gist?**
25. **How have the lessons earned changed the way I think?**

prompts >

literal

Who…
What…
Why…
Where…
When…
How…
Name and define…
List…
Give the reasons why…
Provide support for…

inferential

What do you think…
Why do you think…
I wonder…
What if…
Predict and substantiate…
What do you do when…
What can be exciting about…
What would you do if…
What is your opinion about…
How does this connect with…

analytical

How effectively does the author show, not tell small moment scenes:
Setting?   Action?   Thoughts and Feelings?   Dialogue?

What do you think about the quality of the Traits of Writing:
Ideas?   Organization?   Voice?
Word Choice?   Sentence Fluency?   Conventions?

65

Pillars
of Literacy

Reading

circle
points

five elements of information

elements of information

When we read information text (nonfiction), we learn about our world. We learn about a wide range of subjects for a variety of purposes, identify and understand the main ideas that bring the subject and purpose into focus, and gain important details that add depth to our understanding.

Read an encyclopedia entry or a history book, and you will probably learn something new. Perhaps you will learn about what a steam engine is or about the evolution of smart phones. Every information text addresses a particular subject. There is always a central purpose, which is the reason the author wrote the piece, often for a specific audience. Supporting the subject will be a set of main ideas — important ideas needed to understand the subject and central purpose. There are supporting details — important facts that give a depth of knowledge and understanding to the main ideas. Every information text has these elements in common.

Information is presented through one or more types of text structure:

> description-explanation   > sequence-time   > problem-solution
> persuasive   > cause-effect   > compare-contrast

Recognizing text structures enables us to read for purpose and comprehend.

When we learn to identify and think about information text through its elements and text structure, we are able to make meaning.

subject

a narrowed topic of thought, discussion, investigation, or writing

central purpose

the primary reason an information text has been written; its aim, goal, or objective as made clear by the subject, main ideas, and text structure

main ideas

the important knowledge that contributes to the subject and central purpose of an information text

supporting details

the facts or pieces of information that contribute to understanding a main idea; details add depth to understanding and make a piece of writing more real and interesting; details give life to a description, explain an idea, provide examples, and support a position

text structure

six different types of information text structure, when identified and understood, focus reading accordingly for comprehension:

> description-explanation   > sequence-time   > problem-solution
> persuasive   > cause-effect   > compare-contrast

circle points

five elements of information

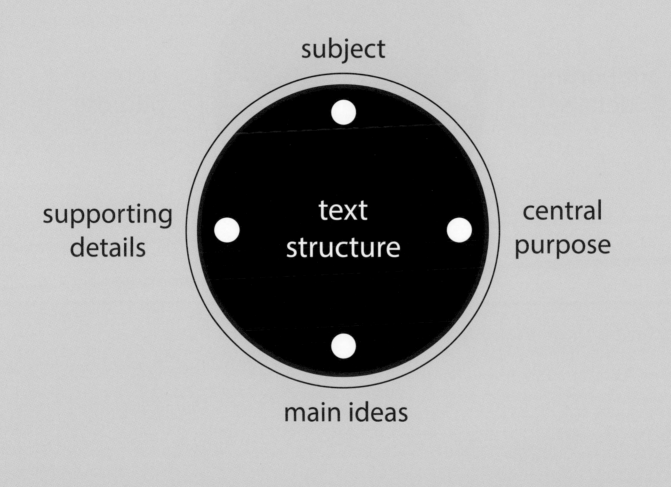

circle
points
five elements of information

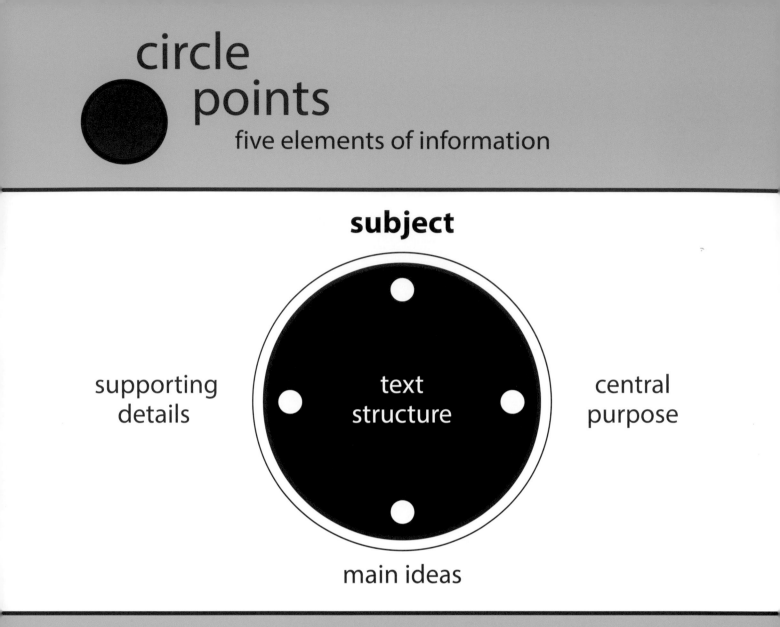

subject

supporting details

text structure

central purpose

main ideas

Enduring Understanding, Essential Question, and the LP

Think About It. Talk About It.
The subject narrows to a topic.

Ask It. Answer It.
Why do we think about the subject?

Learning Points
1. Readers look over the table of contents, read the introduction, and peruse sections and text features of an information text to gain a sense of the subject and topic.
2. Readers think about main ideas and supporting details to understand the subject and central purpose.
3. Readers carry forward main ideas and supporting details as they read in order to interpret and reflect upon the subject and central purpose.

subject

a narrowed topic of thought, discussion, investigation, or writing

questions for meaningful conversation

1. **How would you summarize the subject and topic?**
2. What is the central purpose of this writing? For what audience is it intended?
3. Why do you think this information is important?
4. How might this information change the way people think or act?
5. What does this information tell you about the viewpoint of others?
6. What does this information tell you about yourself?
7. What position would you take regarding this information?
   How would you support your position?
8. How might this information help us solve problems or make decisions?
9. How would you summarize the main ideas that support the subject and topic?
10. What supporting details are important to understand the main ideas? How so?
11. What ideas or details do you disagree with in this piece of writing?
12. What gaps do you see in the content of this writing?
13. What additional ideas and details about this information would you like to learn?
14. What types of text structure are present in this writing? How so?
    - > description–explanation
    - > problem–solution
    - > cause–effect
    - > sequence–time
    - > persuasive
    - > compare–contrast
15. What enduring understandings or essential questions arise from this information?
16. Reading a true story (narrative non-fiction), how would you interpret and reflect upon the main character?
17. Reading a true story (narrative non-fiction), how is it one of achievement, disaster, or both?

literal
Who…
What…
Why…
Where…
When…
How…
Name and define…
List…
Give the reasons why…
Provide support for…

inferential
What do you think…
Why do you think…
I wonder…
What if…
Predict and substantiate…
What do you do when…
What can be exciting about…
What would you do if…
What is your opinion about…
How does this connect with…

analytical
How effectively does the author breathe life into the writing:
Notice?   Think?   Realize?
What do you think about the quality of the Traits of Writing:
Ideas?   Organization?   Voice?
Word Choice?   Sentence Fluency?   Conventions?

circle
points
five elements of information

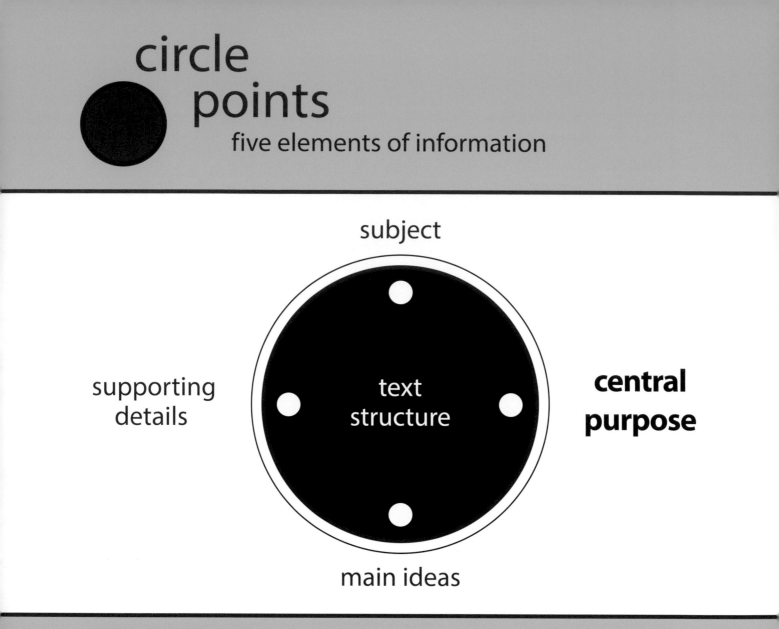

subject

supporting details

text structure

central purpose

main ideas

Enduring Understandings, Essential Questions, and the LP

Think About It. Talk About It.
The central purpose determines position and message.

Ask It. Answer It.
Why do we think about the central purpose?

Learning Points
1. Readers think and grow their understanding of the information's subject, main ideas, and supporting details to determine the author's central purpose.

2. Readers aim to become knowledgeable on an information text's subject and topics to understand the author's purpose.

central purpose

the primary reason an information text has been written;
its aim, goal, or objective as made clear by the subject, main ideas,
and text structure

questions for meaningful conversation

1. How would you summarize the subject and topic?
2. **What is the central purpose of this writing? For what audience is it intended?**
3. **Why do you think this information is important?**
4. **How might this information change the way people think or act?**
5. **What does this information tell you about the viewpoint of others?**
6. **What does this information tell you about yourself?**
7. **What position would you take regarding this information?
   How would you support your position?**
8. **How might this information help us solve problems or make decisions?**
9. How would you summarize the main ideas that support the subject and topic?
10. What supporting details are important to understand the main ideas? How so?
11. What ideas or details do you disagree with in this piece of writing?
12. What gaps do you see in the content of this writing?
13. What additional ideas and details about this information would you like to learn?
14. What types of text structure are present in this writing? How so?
    > description–explanation > problem–solution > cause–effect
    > sequence–time > persuasive > compare–contrast
15. What enduring understandings or essential questions arise from this information?
16. Reading a true story (narrative non-fiction), how would you interpret and reflect
    upon the main character?
17. Reading a true story (narrative non-fiction), how is it one of achievement, disaster, or both?

literal

Who…
What…
Why…
Where…
When…
How…
Name and define…
List…
Give the reasons why…
Provide support for…

inferential

What do you think…
Why do you think…
I wonder…
What if…
Predict and substantiate…
What do you do when…
What can be exciting about…
What would you do if…
What is your opinion about…
How does this connect with…

analytical

How effectively does the author breathe life into the writing:
Notice?   Think?   Realize?
What do you think about the quality of the Traits of Writing:
Ideas?   Organization?   Voice?
Word Choice?   Sentence Fluency?   Conventions?

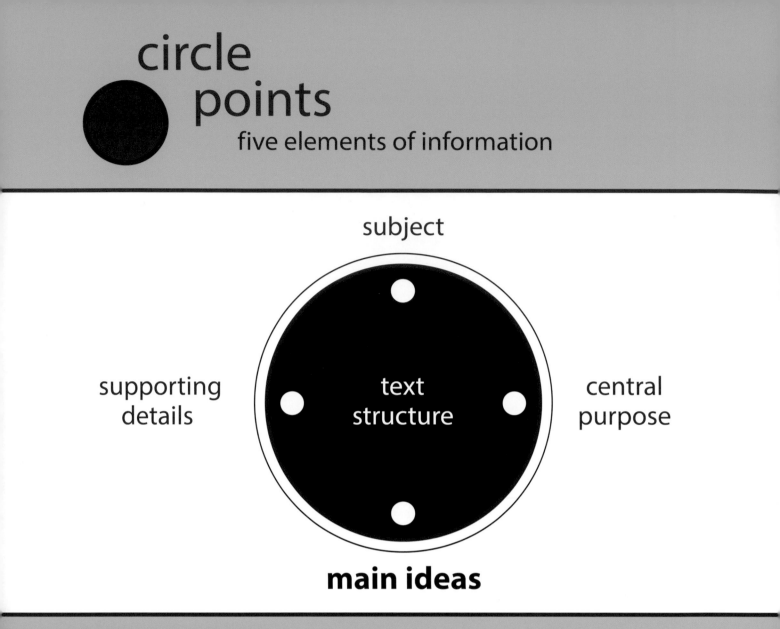

subject

supporting details

text structure

central purpose

main ideas

Enduring Understandings, Essential Questions, and the LP

Think About It. Talk About It.

Main ideas give meaning to the subject and central purpose.

Ask It. Answer It.

Why do we think about the main ideas?

Learning Points

1. Readers think about the main ideas of an information text in relation to the subject and central purpose.
2. Readers read an information text aiming to build knowledge models as experts on a topic; those knowledge models include categories to organize the main ideas and supporting details.
3. Readers read for purpose by identifying main ideas and supporting details, and by carrying forward those ideas and details across text to build and shape understanding.

main ideas

definition >

important knowledge that contributes to the subject
and central purpose of an information text

questions for meaningful conversation

questions >

1. How would you summarize the subject and topic?
2. What is the central purpose of this writing? For what audience is it intended?
3. Why do you think this information is important?
4. How might this information change the way people think or act?
5. What does this information tell you about the viewpoint of others?
6. What does this information tell you about yourself?
7. What position would you take regarding this information?
   How would you support your position?
8. How might this information help us solve problems or make decisions?
9. **How would you summarize the main ideas that support the subject and topic?**
10. What supporting details are important to understand the main ideas? How so?
11. What ideas or details do you disagree with in this piece of writing?
12. What gaps do you see in the content of this writing?
13. What additional ideas and details about this information would you like to learn?
14. What types of text structure are present in this writing? How so?
    - > description–explanation
    - > problem–solution
    - > cause–effect
    - > sequence–time
    - > persuasive
    - > compare–contrast
15. What enduring understandings or essential questions arise from this information?
16. Reading a true story (narrative non-fiction), how would you interpret and reflect upon the main character?
17. Reading a true story (narrative non-fiction), how is it one of achievement, disaster, or both?

prompts >

literal
Who…
What…
Why…
Where…
When…
How…
Name and define…
List…
Give the reasons why…
Provide support for…

inferential
What do you think…
Why do you think…
I wonder…
What if…
Predict and substantiate…
What do you do when…
What can be exciting about…
What would you do if…
What is your opinion about…
How does this connect with…

analytical
How effectively does the author breathe life into the writing:
Notice?   Think?   Realize?
What do you think about the quality of the Traits of Writing:
Ideas?   Organization?   Voice?
Word Choice?   Sentence Fluency?   Conventions?

circle points

five elements of information

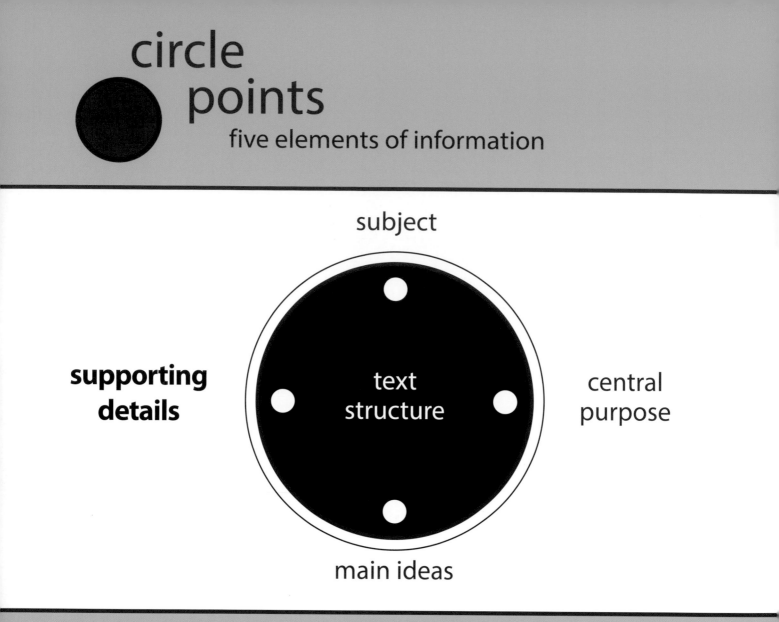

subject

supporting details

text structure

central purpose

main ideas

Enduring Understandings, Essential Questions, and the LP

Think About It. Talk About It.
Supporting details give meaning to main ideas.

Ask It. Answer It.
Why do we think about the supporting details?

Learning Points
1. Readers read information text with the aim of building knowledge models as experts on a topic, and those knowledge models include details they determine to be important to support their understanding of the main ideas.
2. Readers grow and expand their vocabulary of the subject they are reading.
3. Readers think and figure out the meaning of unknown words based upon the context in which they are used.
4. To become knowledgeable on a topic, readers use content vocabulary in order to grow their oral language capacity.

supporting details

the facts or pieces of information that contribute to a main idea; details make a piece of writing more real and interesting; details give life to a description, explain an idea, provide examples, and support an argument

questions for meaningful conversation

1. How would you summarize the subject and topic?
2. What is the central purpose of this writing? For what audience is it intended?
3. Why do you think this information is important?
4. How might this information change the way people think or act?
5. What does this information tell you about the viewpoint of others?
6. What does this information tell you about yourself?
7. What position would you take regarding this information?
   How would you support your position?
8. How might this information help us solve problems or make decisions?
9. How would you summarize the main ideas that support the subject and topic?
10. **What supporting details are important to understand the main ideas? How so?**
11. **What ideas or details do you disagree with in this piece of writing?**
12. **What gaps do you see in the content of this writing?**
13. **What additional ideas and details about this information would you like to learn?**
14. What types of text structure are present in this writing? How so?
    > description–explanation   > problem–solution   > cause–effect
    > sequence–time   > persuasive   > compare–contrast
15. What enduring understandings or essential questions arise from this information?
16. Reading a true story (narrative non-fiction), how would you interpret and reflect upon the main character?
17. Reading a true story (narrative non-fiction), how is it one of achievement, disaster, or both?

literal
Who…
What…
Why…
Where…
When…
How…
Name and define…
List…
Give the reasons why…
Provide support for…

inferential
What do you think…
Why do you think…
I wonder…
What if…
Predict and substantiate…
What do you do when…
What can be exciting about…
What would you do if…
What is your opinion about…
How does this connect with…

analytical
How effectively does the author breathe life into the writing:
Notice?   Think?   Realize?
What do you think about the quality of the Traits of Writing:
Ideas?   Organization?   Voice?
Word Choice?   Sentence Fluency?   Conventions?

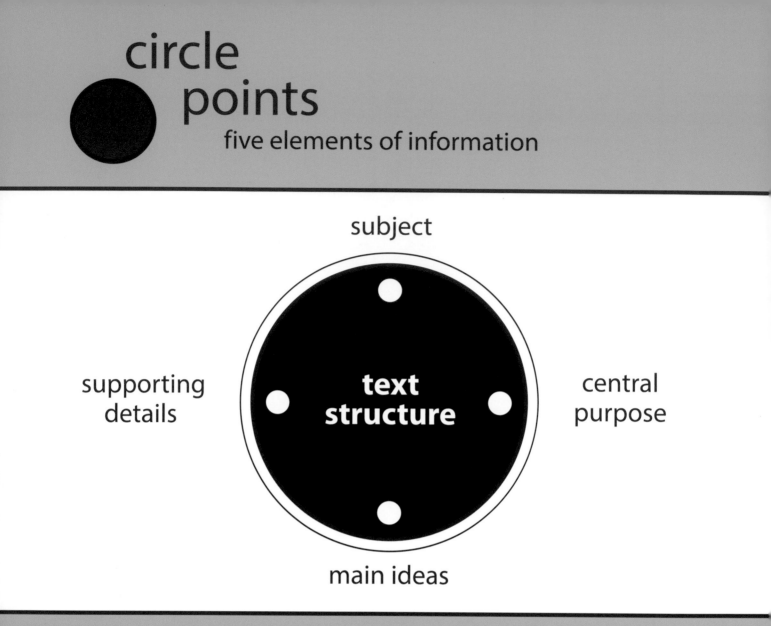

Enduring Understandings, Essential Questions, and the LP

Think About It. Talk About It.
Text structure patterns meaning.

Ask It. Answer It.
Why do we think about text structures?

Learning Points
1. Readers determine the text structure and notice text features to make meaning.
2. Readers identify the text structure of an information text (description-explanation, sequence-time, problem-solution, persuasive, compare-contrast, and/or cause-effect) and focus reading accordingly.
3. Readers use text structure to make and convey meaning.
4. Readers identify enduring understandings and generate essential questions by knowing, understanding, and applying text structure.
5. Readers read true stories (narrative nonfiction) in ways similar to how they read fictional stories, where they interpret and reflect upon a character's desires and struggles.
6. Readers read for purpose and understand that true stories (narrative nonfiction) are often tales of achievement or disaster – both of which have predictable patterns.

text structure

there are six different types of information text structure, when identified and understood, focus reading accordingly for comprehension:

> description-explanation
> persuasive
> sequence-time
> cause-effect
> problem-solution
> compare-contrast

questions for meaningful conversation

1. How would you summarize the subject and topic?
2. What is the central purpose of this writing? For what audience is it intended?
3. Why do you think this information is important?
4. How might this information change the way people think or act?
5. What does this information tell you about the viewpoint of others?
6. What does this information tell you about yourself?
7. What position would you take regarding this information?
   How would you support your position?
8. How might this information help us solve problems or make decisions?
9. How would you summarize the main ideas that support the subject and topic?
10. What supporting details are important to understand the main ideas? How so?
11. What ideas or details do you disagree with in this piece of writing?
12. What gaps do you see in the content of this writing?
13. What additional ideas and details about this information would you like to learn?
14. **What types of text structure are present in this writing? How so?**
    > **description–explanation**
    > **sequence–time**
    > **problem–solution**
    > **persuasive**
    > **cause–effect**
    > **compare–contrast**
15. **What enduring understandings or essential questions arise from this information?**
16. **Reading a true story (narrative non-fiction), how would you interpret and reflect upon the main character?**
17. **Reading a true story (narrative non-fiction), how is it one of achievement, disaster, or both?**

literal
Who…
What…
Why…
Where…
When…
How…
Name and define…
List…
Give the reasons why…
Provide support for…

inferential
What do you think…
Why do you think…
I wonder…
What if…
Predict and substantiate…
What do you do when…
What can be exciting about…
What would you do if…
What is your opinion about…
How does this connect with…

analytical
How effectively does the author breathe life into the writing:
Notice?   Think?   Realize?
What do you think about the quality of the Traits of Writing:
Ideas?   Organization?   Voice?
Word Choice?   Sentence Fluency?   Conventions?

Pillars
of Literacy

Writing

traits of writing

six traits of writing

traits of writing

There are two basic types of writing: narrative (story) and non-narrative (information). Writing narrative or non-narrative, we aim to produce good writing. We define good writing with six traits.

We use ideas and details in order to entertain, inform, and persuade. We focus on organization so that there is a logical sequence and order. We say every day things in creative ways – a distinctive voice helps the reader feel that a real person is behind the words. We consider word choice, using words that are precise to communicate exactly what we mean to say. We write with sentence fluency so that writing has a rhythm and is easy to read. Prior to publication, we are sure that the conventions of our writing are error-free.

These are the six Traits of Writing. When we name and identify good writing with the six Traits of Writing we learn to evaluate writing as a habit of mind. We notice the six Traits of Writing when we read, and we apply the Traits when we write. As we learn to read through the eyes of a writer and to write keeping the six Traits of Writing in mind, we make the reading - writing connection. We grow our ability to become a passionate and confident writer.

Sharing a common language and understanding of a standard set of terms to identify good writing, we strengthen our ability to learn to write well.

traits of
writing

six traits of writing

traits of writing

1. **Ideas**
   Produce writing rich with ideas and details to give depth to meaning.

2. **Organization**
   Structure writing in a logical sequence with a beginning, middle, and end (narrative) or introduction, body, and conclusion (non-narrative).

3. **Voice**
   Create an original flavor and personal tone in writing.

4. **Word Choice**
   Use precise, accurate, and colorful vocabulary to convey meaning.

5. **Sentence Fluency**
   Craft sentences with a natural rhythm and cadence.

6. **Conventions**
   Edit for mechanical correctness - spelling, punctuation, capitalization, and grammar.

analytical comprehension

We learn to write as we read by looking at a piece of writing not just as a reader, but also through the eyes of a writer to appreciate the writer's craft.

As a reader and a writer, we evaluate the quality of the writing using the six Traits of Writing. We refer to this as analytical comprehension.

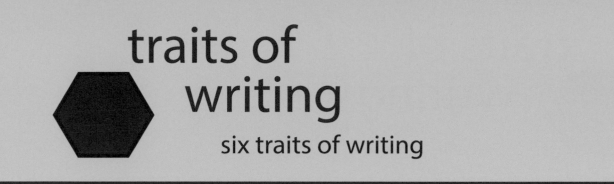

traits of
writing

six traits of writing

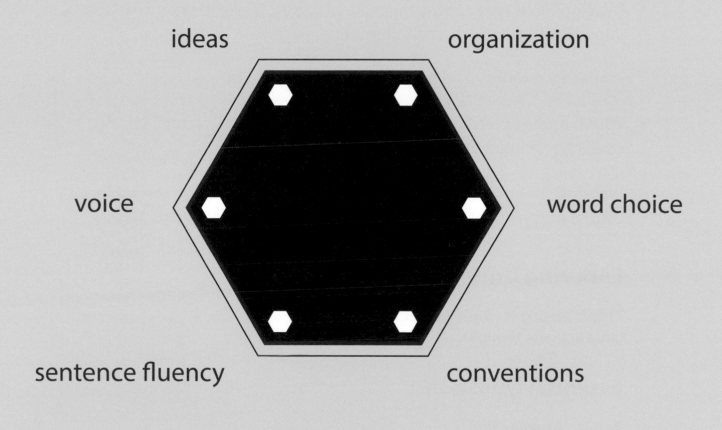

ideas

organization

voice

word choice

sentence fluency

conventions

traits of writing
ideas

1. Ideas

Produce writing rich with ideas and details to give depth to meaning.

Develop ideas that convey the main message. Make ideas and details interesting, important, and informative.

Produce a quantity and quality of ideas and details.

Within a story, craft ideas and details through the characters, setting, conflict, resolution, and plot.

Within an information text, craft ideas and details through the subject, central purpose, main ideas, supporting details, and text structure.

Enduring Understanding

Think About It. Talk About It.
Ideas activate thought.

Essential Question

Ask It. Answer It.
Why do we write with ideas and details?

Learning Point
1. Writers produce stories (narrative writing) and information (non-narrative) rich with ideas and details.

2. Organization

Structure writing in a logical sequence with a beginning, middle, and end (narrative) or introduction, body, and conclusion (non-narrative).

Use the different types of text structure to guide organization.

Use the different types of text features purposefully to enhance organization.

Within a story, craft a well sequenced plot (exposition, rising action, climax, falling action, and resolution).

Within an information text, craft a well developed boxes and bullets outline (thesis/introduction, topic sentences, supporting details, and conclusion).

Enduring Understanding

Think About It. Talk About It.
Organization logically sequences meaning.

Essential Question

Ask It. Answer It.
Why do we write with organization?

Learning Points
1. Writers plan story (narrative) or information (non-narrative) writing with a logical and sequenced organization. They use plot lines and outlines to guide their writing.
2. Writers use text structures and text features purposefully to guide and enhance organization.

3. Voice

Create an original flavor and personal tone in writing.

Develop a unique style of writing. Enable the reader to feel that a real person is behind the words. Write with emotion and energy. Find creative ways to say everyday things. Develop a mature command of the language. Understand and use figurative language, but avoid clichés.

1. **Simile:** comparing two unlike things using like or as
   The yard, full of fireflies, sparkled like a thousand stars in the night.

2. **Metaphor:** comparing two unlike things without using like or as
   The Internet is a highway of information.

3. **Personification:** a thing, place, or idea given qualities of a person
   The beauty of the painting spoke to my soul.

4. **Hyperbole:** an exaggerated comparison
   The tree was so tall it touched the clouds.

5. **Alliteration:** the repetition of sounds at the beginning of words
   Grandpa grabbed the green grapes right from the vine.

Enduring Understanding

Think About It. Talk About It.
Voice brings originality.

Essential Question

Ask It. Answer It.
Why do we write with voice?

Learning Point
1. Writers aim to write with voice in order to be original in what they write with a style all their own.

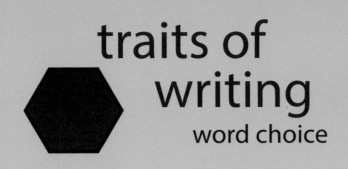

4. Word Choice

Use precise, accurate, and colorful vocabulary to convey meaning.

Determine the best words to show meaning. Carefully choose words to paint a picture in the reader's mind and stimulate the senses — use precise nouns, descriptive adjectives, strong verbs, and illustrative adverbs. Aim to use just the right word in the right place and at the right time.

Develop a broad and ever-expanding vocabulary. Know that word choice is not just the use of a broad vocabulary. It is the ability to use words in an effective way.

Enduring Understanding

Think About It. Talk About It.
Word choice conveys precise and accurate meaning.

Essential Question

Ask It. Answer It.
Why do we write with word choice?

Learning Points
1. Writers use precise, accurate, and colorful words to convey meaning.
2. Writers demonstrate effective and accurate word choice with precise nouns, descriptive adjectives, strong verbs, and illustrative adverbs.

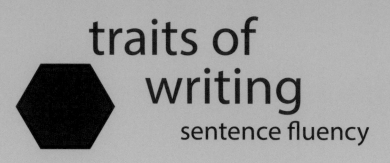

5. Sentence Fluency

Craft sentences with a natural rhythm and cadence.

Think about how writing sounds when read aloud. Know that sentence fluency is evident when the writing is easy to read with expression and pace.

Revise sentences that are awkward to read. Use a variety of sentence types, which flow together naturally. Craft sentences with a variety of beginnings and varied length.

Avoid sentence fragments and run-on sentences unless used purposely for effect.

Enduring Understanding

Think About It. Talk About It.
Sentence fluency enables expression and pace.

Essential Question

Ask It. Answer It.
Why do we write with sentence fluency?

Learning Points
1. Writers craft sentences with a natural, smooth fluency.
2. Writers craft sentences with a natural variety of beginnings and lengths; simple and complex sentences are used.

6. Conventions

Edit for mechanical correctness — spelling, punctuation, capitalization, and grammar.   Apply the standard rules of the English language.

Know that a piece of writing with error-free conventions is the result of a knowledge and understanding of the rules, thorough proofreading, and strong editing skills.

Realize that handwriting and neatness are not considered part of conventions.

Enduring Understanding

Think About It. Talk About It.
Conventions make writing readable.

Essential Question

Ask It. Answer It.
Why do we write with conventions?

Learning Point
1. Writers publish writing with error-free conventions.
2. Writers edit spelling, punctuation, capitalization, and grammar.

Pillars
of Literacy

Writing

writing
strategies

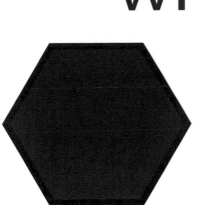

two writing strategies

writing strategies

First and foremost, writers aim to develop and exercise writing fluency; in other words, we strive to write freely, getting our ideas down on paper. We do not worry about spelling and other conventions, but rather focus on expressing our ideas and experiences as a stream of thoughts.

There are two effective strategies we use to develop writing fluency for narrative (story) and non-narrative (information) writing.

Writing narrative, we zoom in on small moment scenes. We aim to show, not tell the setting, action, thoughts and feelings, and dialogue in order to create movies in the mind of the reader. To quote Anton Chekhov, "Don't tell me the moon is shining; show me the glint of light on broken glass."

Writing non-narravive, we breathe life into reports and essays by not only supporting the subject or thesis with ideas and details, but with anecdotal stories and by expressing what we notice, think, and realize. To quote Edward Tutfe, "The point of the essay is to change things." When we inform and educate and express our thoughts, we change the way people think.

1. Small Moment Scene

Develop narrative writing fluency by stretching a small moment to show, not tell the setting, action, thoughts and feelings, and dialogue.

Zoom in to help the reader to visualize sensual and emotional imagery, bringing them into the imaginary world of the story and to walk in the shoes of the character.

Enduring Understanding

Think About It. Talk About It.
Small moment scenes form mental and emotional imagery.

Essential Question

Ask It. Answer It.
Why do we write small moment scenes?

Learning Points
1. Crafting small moment scenes, writers stretch the moment by showing, not telling the setting, action, thoughts and feelings, and dialogue to paint vivid movies in the mind of the reader.

2. Notice, Think, Realize

Develop non-narrative writing fluency by expressing what we notice, think, and realize.

See more, hear more, smell more, taste more, and feel more.
Move readers to pause, think, and see in new ways.

Enduring Understanding

Think About It. Talk About It.
Notice, think, and realize patterns of expression grow insight and reflection.

Essential Question

Ask It. Answer It.
Why do we write what we notice, think, and realize?

Learning Points
1. Writers observe the world around them, and express themselves in writing through the following prompts: *I notice… This makes me think… Now I realize…*
2. Writers see more, hear more, smell more, taste more, and feel more.

Pillars
of Literacy

Writing

primary forms of writing

five primary forms of writing

primary forms of writing

Writers know that five of the most common and important forms of writing are the personal narrative, short story, report, essay and persuasive essay.

The personal narrative and short story are forms of narrative writing. Character, setting, conflict, resolution, and plot are primary elements of these forms of writing. When we write a personal narrative, we think in terms of a beginning, middle, and end. When we write a short story, we think in terms of exposition, rising action, climax, falling action, and resolution (the plot). Within the personal narrative or short story, we focus on showing small moment scenes (setting, action, thoughts & feelings, and dialogue), aiming to create movies in the mind of the reader.

The report, essay, and persuasive essay are forms of non-narrative writing. The subject, central purpose, main ideas, supporting details, and text structure are primary elements of these forms of writing. When we write a report or essay, we think in terms of an introduction, body, and conclusion. Writing a report or essay, we work through a boxes and bullets outline, aiming to support the thesis with topic sentences and supporting details, including reflecting upon what we notice, think, and realize.

First Steps to Writing

As we learn to write and apply our skills as a writer, a first step is to develop writing fluency. What is writing fluency?

Writing fluency is a flowing and seemingly effortless use of language in writing. It is our ability to write freely and continuously, expressing our ideas and thoughts. We are fluent writers when there is a natural organization to our written work.

One of the biggest challenges for us to get started as writers is demonstrated by comments such as, "I don't know how to start," and "I'm not sure where to begin," and "I don't know what to write." The best way to become a fluent writer is to use strategies that help us to write without concern for what is right or wrong, having no worries about conventions such as spelling, punctuation, capitalization, or grammar. (Conventions, though important, are better left for the revising and editing phases of the writing process.)

Enduring Understanding

Think About It. Talk About It.
Writing fluency enables the expression of thoughts and ideas.

Essential Question

Ask It. Answer It.
Why do we write fluently?

primary forms of writing
first steps to writing

Learning Points

1. Writers know that writing fluency (freely and continuously) is a first step to learning to express thoughts and ideas.

2. Writers know that conversation feeds writing. By first engaging in conversation about their thoughts and ideas, they prepare to write with fluency.

3. Writers log seed ideas in a journal, returning in search of one that they care about and can stretch into a personal narrative, story, report, or essay.

4. Writers exercise fluency by writing about first times, last times, or times when they realized something important.

5. Writers exercise fluency by writing about personal experiences linked to a specific emotion.

6. Writing small moment scenes is a first step to developing fluency for narrative writing. Writers zoom in and stretch the moment aiming to show, not tell the setting, action, thoughts and feelings, and dialogue.

7. Writing in response to the world around us is a first step to developing fluency for non-narrative writing. Writers observe the world through the eyes of a writer by seeing more, hearing more, smelling more, tasting more, and feeling more. They write to the prompts: I notice, I think, I realize.

8. Writers share their work through conversation, aiming to coach one another and get constructive feedback per the six Traits of Writing, small moment scenes, and expressing what they notice, think, and realize.

1. Personal Narrative

A personal narrative tells the story of a moment or event we have experienced in life. It could be a special memory we will never forget. It could be something that happened recently. The moments and events in our lives are part of the universal human experience.

The personal narrative is one of the first forms of writing we learn as we develop the ability to write. We are able to develop our writing fluency through personal narratives because we are knowledgeable when we write about ourselves. We are the experts on our lives.

When we write about our own experience, we tell a story. We strive to make the story engaging for the reader by showing, not telling, and stretching small moment scenes by zooming in on the setting, action, thoughts and feelings, and dialogue.

Enduring Understanding

Think About It. Talk About It.
Personal narrative writing reflects the universal human experience.

Essential Question

Ask It. Answer It.
Why do we write a personal narrative?

primary forms of writing

personal narrative learning points

Learning Points

1. Writers know and understand that the personal narrative tells a story of something they have experienced in life.
2. Writers get ideas for writing personal narratives by paying attention to and reflecting upon the events and issues in their lives.
3. Writers log seed ideas for a personal narrative focusing on a special person, place, object, and/or event in their lives.
4. Writers log seed ideas in a journal, returning in search of one that they care about and can stretch into a personal narrative.
5. Writers think about what direction to stretch a seed idea, considering several possibilities.
6. Writers plan to write a personal narrative by outlining small moment scene ideas in a sequence of events – the beginning, middle, and end.
7. Writers draft small moment scenes, aiming to show, not tell the setting, action, thoughts and feelings, and dialogue.
8. Writers draft leads that hook the reader.
9. Writers draft small moment scenes across the beginning, middle, and end.
10. Writers make effective use of transition words and phrases to move from one small moment scene to the next.
11. Writers draft endings that provoke thinking (i.e., a question or surprise ending).
12. Writers study personal narratives, comparing and contrasting the quality of writing in terms of the six Traits of Writing and how effectively the author stretches small moment scenes.

2. Short Story

A short story is a work of fiction. Fiction is writing about imagined events and characters.

The short story explores the human experience across cultures and throughout history. A short story will typically concentrate on a single event with only one or two characters.

The literary elements of a short story are characters, setting, conflict, resolution, and plot. The plot, or story mountain, includes the exposition, rising action, climax, falling action, and resolution.

A short story has a theme, including a message – the gist.

Enduring Understanding

Think About It. Talk About It.
Short story writing explores the human experience across cultures and throughout history.

Essential Question

Ask It. Answer It.
Why do we write a short story?

primary forms
of writing
short story learning points

Learning Points

1. Writers know that a short story is a work of fiction. Fiction is writing about imagined events and characters. A short story will typically concentrate on a single event with only one or two characters.

2. Writers get ideas for writing short stories by paying attention and reflecting upon the events and issues in their lives and the world around them.

3. Writers log seed ideas in a journal, returning in search of one that they care about and can stretch into a short story.

4. Writers think about what direction to stretch a seed idea for a short story, considering several possibilities.

5. Writers plan short stories by deciding upon a theme, message, and/or life lesson.

6. Writers plan short stories with a story line (who did what, why, and the conflict).

7. Writers plan short stories by developing character sketches, detailing a character's internal personality traits and external physical traits.

8. Writers plan short stories by developing the character's desires and struggles.

9. Writers plan short stories by outlining ideas for small moment scenes ideas across a plot line (story mountain).

10. Writers draft small moment scenes to introduce the characters, setting, and background knowledge to set a short story's events in motion. This is the exposition of a story.

11. Writers draft small moment scenes to show the character's desires and struggles. The character's personality traits are made evident in response to events. The conflict of the story unfolds. This is the rising action of a short story.

12. Writers draft small moment scenes to show the turning point of a story. The character faces the high point of the conflict. This is the climax of a short story.

13. Writers draft small moment scenes to move a story towards the end by showing how the character has changed and by resolving the unresolved difficulties. This is the falling action of a short story.

14. Writers draft small moment scenes to finish a story with a natural, thought-provoking, and/or surprise ending to the story, and in doing so deliver the story's message. This is the resolution of a short story.

15. Writers make effective use of transition words and phrases to move from one small moment scene to the next.

16. Writers study short stories, comparing and contrasting the quality of writing in terms of the six Traits of Writing and how effectively the author stretches small moment scenes.

3. Report

A report is a non-narrative work of nonfiction.

A report is written to record events or to inform and educate an audience about a subject and topic.   It is meant to present information on a subject factually and objectively.

One or more of the six basic text structures are used:

> description-explanation   > sequence-time   > problem-solution
> persuasive   > cause-effect   > compare-contrast

Enduring Understanding

Think About It. Talk About It.
Report writing informs and educates.

Essential Question

Ask It. Answer It.
Why do we write a report?

primary forms of writing

report learning points

Learning Points

1. Writers know and understand that a report is a non-narrative work of nonfiction. A report is written to record events or to inform and educate an audience about a subject.

2. Writers reference books as models to learn how authors write a report.

3. Writers log seed ideas in a journal, returning in search of one that they care about and can stretch into a report.

4. Writers think about what direction to stretch a seed idea for a report, considering several possibilities.

5. Writers plan reports by first determining the subject and central purpose with the aim of narrowing the topic.

6. Writers plan reports by collecting/researching ideas and details to determine what is most important to inform and educate the reader about their chosen subject and topic.

7. Writers plan reports by determining which text structures best serve the purpose of their writing:
   > description-explanation > sequence-time > problem-solution
   > persuasive > cause-effect > compare-contrast

8. Writers plan reports by developing a table of contents to determine how the information text might be organized.

9. Writers plan reports by developing a boxes and bullets outline.

10. Writers draft reports by starting with the ideas, sections, and chapters we know something about.

11. Writers draft an introduction that effectively presents the subject and central purpose, important background knowledge, and compels the reader to engage in reading.

12. Writers draft a body with several sections, each presenting a main idea followed by important supporting details.

13. Writers make effective use of transition words and phrases, including text features, to move from one section or idea to the next.

14. Writers draft conclusions that summarize the subject and main ideas to enable the reader to gain enduring understandings and reflect.

4. Essay

An essay is a non-narrative piece of nonfiction.

Essays describe, clarify, argue, and analyze a single topic. An essay can be informative or persuasive. An essay includes an introduction, thesis statement, body, and conclusion. It is a short composition.

An introductory paragraph presents an issue focused by a position, which is the thesis statement.

The body of the essay has several paragraphs, each having a topic sentence and supporting details to demonstrate and/or prove the thesis statement. The topic sentence presents the main idea of a paragraph and supports the thesis statement. The supporting details demonstrate the topic sentence and include important facts, examples, evidence, anecdotal stories, and what we notice, think, and realize.

One or more of the six basic text structures are applied:

> description-explanation   > sequence-time   > problem-solution
> persuasive   > cause-effect   > compare-contrast

A conclusion restates the thesis statement (the position), and leaves the reader with a sense of importance for the topic and ideas.

Enduring Understanding

Think About It. Talk About It.
Essay writing describes, clarifies, argues, or analyzes a thesis.

Essential Question

Ask It. Answer It.
Why do we write an essay?

primary forms of writing

essay learning points

Learning Points

1. Writers know that an essay is a non-narrative piece of non-fiction, and that essays are written to inform, educate, and change the thinking of the reader.
2. Writers log seed ideas in a journal, returning in search of one that they care about and can stretch into an essay.
3. Writers think about what direction to stretch a seed idea for an essay, considering several possibilities.
4. Writers plan an essay by choosing one idea they feel strongly about. They draft it in different ways to gain clarity of the position they want to take. This is the thesis.
5. Writers plan an essay by developing a list of main ideas to support the thesis.
6. Writers plan an essay by developing lists of important details to support a main idea.
7. Writers draft an essay's introduction with the thesis statement and an overview of the main ideas and important background information.
8. Writers draft an essay's body paragraphs, each with a topic sentence, which is a main idea supporting the thesis.
9. Writers draft supporting details for each topic sentence, such as important facts, evidence, and examples.
10. Writers draft supporting details for each topic sentence, such as anecdotal stories.
11. Writers draft supporting details for each topic sentence by expressing what they notice, think, and realize.
12. Writers draft a conclusion to restate the thesis, and to leave the reader with a sense of importance for the thesis and main ideas.
13. Writers use a "boxes and bullets" outline to plan and draft an essay:

THESIS STATEMENT AND INTRODUCTION (Claim or Position)
TOPIC SENTENCE (Main Idea Supporting the Claim or Position)
 • SUPPORTING DETAILS – FACTS, EXAMPLES, EVIDENCE
 • SUPPORTING DETAILS – ANECDOTAL STORIES
 • SUPPORTING DETAILS – I NOTICE, I THINK, I REALIZE
TOPIC SENTENCE (Main Idea Supporting the Claim or Position)
 • SUPPORTING DETAILS – FACTS, EXAMPLES, EVIDENCE
 • SUPPORTING DETAILS – ANECDOTAL STORIES
 • SUPPORTING DETAILS – I NOTICE, I THINK, I REALIZE
TOPIC SENTENCE (Main Idea Supporting the Claim or Position)
 • SUPPORTING DETAILS – FACTS, EXAMPLES, EVIDENCE
 • SUPPORTING DETAILS – ANECDOTAL STORIES
 • SUPPORTING DETAILS – I NOTICE, I THINK, I REALIZE
CLOSING AND RESTATEMENT OF THESIS

5. Persuasive Essay

A persuasive essay states a position with the aim of convincing the reader what he or she should believe. Essential questions that drive a persuasive essay include:

Why is this right or wrong?   Why and how do we need to change?

An introductory paragraph presents the issue focused by a position, which is the thesis statement. Meaningful background information is included in the introduction, with the aim of introducing the agrument for persuading the reader to change their thinking.

The body of the persuasive essay has several paragraphs, each having a topic sentence and supporting details to demonstrate and/or prove the thesis statement. The supporting details may include facts, examples, evidence, anecdotal stories, and what we notice, think, and realize. One or more of the six basic text structures are applied:

> description-explanation   > sequence-time   > problem-solution
> persuasive   > cause-effect   > compare-contrast

The conclusion restates the thesis statement, and urges the reader to change their thinking, accept the position, and/or take action.

Enduring Understanding

Think About It. Talk About It.
Persuasive essay writing changes thinking.

Essential Question

Ask It. Answer It.
Why do we write a persuasive essay?

primary forms of writing

persuasive essay learning points

Learning Points

1. Writers know that a persuasive essay states a position, with the aim of convincing the reader what he or she should believe. Essential questions that drive a persuasive essay include:

    Why is this right or wrong?   Why and how do we need to change?

2. Writers use the same strategies to write persuasive essays that they use to write an informative essay, but they know the primary purpose is to change the thinking of the reader, convincing them to believe the position they argue.

3. Writers plan a persuasive essay by listing reasons why they are right and why the reader should agree in order to support their argument.

4. Writers plan a persuasive essay by researching and collecting undisputable facts and evidence to support their argument.

5. Writers draft a persuasive essay in the same way they draft an informative essay.

6. Writers revise the persuasive essay draft, looking to fill holes and gaps in the argument.

7. Writers revise the persuasive essay draft, rereading again and again, imagining how the reader might not be persuaded. They make revisions to strengthen the argument.

8. Writers use a "boxes and bullets" outline to plan and draft a persuasive essay:

THESIS STATEMENT AND INTRODUCTION (Claim or Position)
TOPIC SENTENCE (Main Idea Supporting the Claim or Position)
   • SUPPORTING DETAILS – FACTS, EXAMPLES, EVIDENCE
   • SUPPORTING DETAILS – ANECDOTAL STORIES
   • SUPPORTING DETAILS – I NOTICE, I THINK, I REALIZE
TOPIC SENTENCE (Main Idea Supporting the Claim or Position)
   • SUPPORTING DETAILS – FACTS, EXAMPLES, EVIDENCE
   • SUPPORTING DETAILS – ANECDOTAL STORIES
   • SUPPORTING DETAILS – I NOTICE, I THINK, I REALIZE
TOPIC SENTENCE (Main Idea Supporting the Claim or Position)
   • SUPPORTING DETAILS – FACTS, EXAMPLES, EVIDENCE
   • SUPPORTING DETAILS – ANECDOTAL STORIES
   • SUPPORTING DETAILS – I NOTICE, I THINK, I REALIZE
CLOSING AND RESTATEMENT OF THESIS

Pillars
of Literacy

Writing

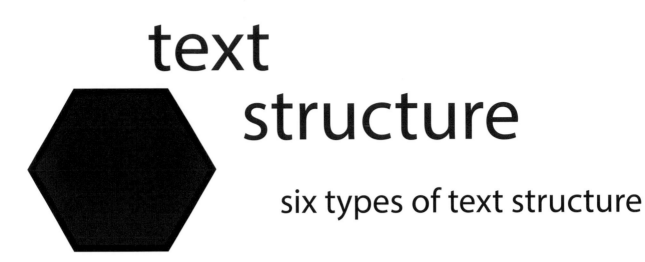

text structure

six types of text structure

types of text structure

Information text has one or more types of text structure based upon the author's purpose:

1. Description-Explanation
2. Sequence-Time
3. Problem-Solution
4. Persuasive
5. Cause-Effect
6. Compare-Contrast

When writers use one or more of the six types of text structure to inform and educate an audience about a subject, it enables readers to make meaning.

1. Description-Explanation

A description text structure shows mental images of the details of an event, person, place, or object.

An explanation text structure shows a set of facts, which clarify the context, causes, and consequences of those facts.

Features of Description-Explanation

- Details about person, place, object, and/or event
- Sensory description - what is heard, seen, smelled, tasted, felt
- Precise use of adjectives
- Figurative language: similes, metaphors, personification, hyperbole
- Strong development of the experience that puts the reader there
- Questions posed include:
  What story, event, person, place or object is being described?
  How is it being described (what does it look like, how does it work, etc.)?
  What is important to remember?
- Signal words and phrases:
  for instance,...
  such as...
  to begin with,...
  to illustrate...
  characteristics include...

Learning Point
1. Crafting a description text structure, writers show images and details of an event, person, place, or object focused on the who or what did what, where, when, why, and how.
2. Crafting an explanation text structure, writers show an account of facts and clarify reasons and justifications for the causes and consequences of those facts.

2. Sequence-Time

A sequence-time text structure describes or explains how things happen or work in chronological order.

Features of Sequence-Time

- Details describing or explaining the order of what happened
- Questions pondered include:
  What items, events, or steps are listed?
  Do they have to happen in this order?
  Do they always happen in this order?
- Signal words and phrases:
  first,
  second,
  next,
  then,
  before,
  after,
  finally,
  following...
  not long after...
  now,
  soon,

Learning Point
1. Crafting a time-sequence text structure, writers show a detailed, chronological account of how something happens, how to do something, or how to make something.

3. Problem-Solution

A problem-solution text structure presents a problem, including why there is a problem, followed by one or more possible solutions.

Features of Problem-Solution

- Statements of what is the problem
- Statements of why the problem exists
- Statements of what is being done to solve the problem
- Statements of how the problem might be solved
- Questions posed include:
  What is the problem?
  Why is this a problem?
  Is anything being done to solve the problem?
  What can be done to solve the problem?
- Signal words and phrases:
  The question is...
  The dilemma is...
  The puzzle is...
  One reason for the problem is...
  To solve this...
  One answer is...

Learning Point

1. Crafting a problem-solution text structure, writers show a detailed description or explanation of the problem followed by proposed solutions to the problem.

4. Persuasive

A persuasive text structure states a position and argues a reason, or set of reasons, in support of the position with the aim of persuading the reader that an action or idea is right or wrong.

Features of Persuasive

- A position statement at the beginning (thesis statement)
- A logical sequence of points with supporting evidence
- Shows cause and effect
- A summing up or restating of the position at the end
- Repetition of words, phrases, and concepts for effect in support of the thesis
- Strong adjectives, verbs, adverbs, and emotive language
- Thought provoking questions:
  What is the purpose of this?
  Why do we allow this to happen?
  How can we change?
- Signal words and phrases:
  We must...
  If we don't...
  It's crucial...
- Types of Arguments:
  To plead a case
  To promote or sell goods and services
  To put forward an argument

Learning Points
1. Crafting a persuasive text structure, writers take a position on an issue and justify it to persuade the reader to change their thinking.
2. Crafting a persuasive text structure, writers show a logical sequence of reasoning and evidence to justify a position.

5. Cause-Effect

A cause and effect text structure shows the connection between what has happened and its impact or result.   Cause is what happened.   Effect is the resulting action or consequence.

Features of Cause-Effect

- Details and specifics as to what has happened and the resulting effects
- Questions pondered include:
  What happened?
  What caused it to happen?
  What is the result?
- Signal words and phrases:
  So,...
  Because...
  Since...
  Therefore...
  If..., then...
  This led to...
  The reason why...
  As a result,
  This may be due to...
  The effect of...
  Consequently,...
  For this reason,...

Learning Point
1. Crafting a cause-effect text structure, writers show a description and explanation of an event or happening and make the connection to resulting actions and effects.

6. Compare-Contrast

A compare and contrast text structure shows how two or more things are alike and/or how they are different.

Features of Compare-Contrast

- Details of similarities and differences between two or more persons, places, or objects
- Questions posed include:
  What things are being compared?
  In what ways are they alike?
  In what ways are they different?
- Signal words and phrases:
  Similar...
  As well as...
  Not only..., but also...
  Both...
  Instead of...
  Either..., or...
  On the other hand,...
  Different from...
  As opposed to...

Learning Point
1. Crafting a compare-contrast text structure, writers show descriptions between two or more persons, places, or objects, and highlight the similarities and differences.

Pillars
of Literacy

Writing

genres and features

fourteen types of genres and features

fourteen types of genres and features

A genre is a type of composition in literature, characterized by similarities in text forms, text structure, text features, and subject matter.

narrative nonfiction
1. biography
2. autobiography

non-narrative nonfiction
3. report
4. essay
5. directions
6. instructions

narrative fiction
7. realistic fiction
8. historical fiction
9. science fiction
10. fantasy
11. fairy tales and fables
12. mystery
13. myth
14. horror

1. Biography

Features of a Biography

Why do we write biographies?
- To chronicle a person's life
- To publicize a person or perpetuate the memory of a person
- To acknowledge a person's influence and contributions

What are biographies?
- Narrative works of nonfiction — an account of a person's life with an emphasis on character, career, and achievements
- An accurate history of a person's life, including the time and place in which he or she lived

Forms and features of biographies:
- Book, article, excerpt
- Details of the person's life: childhood, education, relationships, and achievements
- Research and facts
- Photographs, quotations, and comments from others about the person

Biography Mentor Texts

Lower Level
The Story of Ruby Bridges by Robert Coles
Snowflake Bentley by Jacqueline Briggs
The Fossil Girl: Mary Annings' Dinosaur Discovery by Catherine Brighton

Upper Level
I Was Born a Slave: The Story of Harriet Jacobs by Jennifer Fleischner
The Tree of Life by Peter Sis
Charles A. Lindbergh: A Human Hero by James C. Giblin

Learning Point
1. Know, understand, and apply features of a biography to make meaning as a reader and convey meaning as a writer.

2. Autobiography

Features of an Autobiography

Why do we write autobiographies?
- To record personal achievements, influences, and reflections about our own life
- To record information about our personality, interests, and opinions about life

What are autobiographies?
- Narrative works of nonfiction — a first-person account of one's life

Forms and features of autobiographies:
- Book, article, excerpt
- Information about the world during the life of the author
- Subjective accounts of events

Autobiography Mentor Texts

Lower Level
26 Fairmount Avenue by Tomie DePaola
Mei Fuh: Memories from China by Edith Schaeffer
Thank you, Mr. Faulkner by Particia Polacco

Upper Level
Looking Back: A Book of Memories by Lois Lowery
The Abracadabra Kid: A Writer's Life by Sid Fleischman
Boy: Tales of Childhood by Roald Dahl

Learning Point
1. Know, understand, and apply features of an autobiography to make meaning as a reader and convey meaning as a writer.

3. Report

Features of a Report

Why do we write reports?
- To record events, research, decisions, or progress on a task
- To present information on a subject, factually and objectively

What is a report?
- Non-narrative works of nonfiction that informs and educates about a subject
- A written account of a subject, events, research, and/or decisions

Forms and features of reports:
- Newspaper or magazine piece of writing, nonfiction book, professional journal, research paper, travel book, consumer report, television news presentation
- Subject and purpose established in an opening statement
- Introduction, body, and conclusion
- Written in past tense
- Includes summaries, main ideas, supporting details, facts, and references

Report Mentor Texts
Lower Level
The Life Cycle of Emperor Penguins by Bobbie Kalman
Cactus Hotel by Brenda Guiberson
Secrets of Mummies by Harriet Griffey

Upper Level
Can It Rain Cats and Dogs: Questions and Answers by Melvin Berger
Ancient Aztecs by Henrey Russell
A Negro League Scrapbook by Carole Boston Weatherford

Learning Point
1. Know, understand, and apply features of a report to make meaning as a reader and convey meaning as a writer.

4. Essay

Features of an Essay

Why do we write essays?
- To explain, explore, or argue ideas on a single topic

What are essays?
- Non-narrative works of non-fiction
- A short composition on a topic or theme, explained and supported by evidence

Forms and features of essays:
- Newspaper viewpoint or opinion article
- Introduction presents a position (thesis statement)
- Body paragraphs support the thesis (topic sentences and supporting details)
- One or more text structures: description-explanation, sequence-time, problem-solution, persuasive, cause-effect, and compare-contrast
- The closing paragraph(s) restates the thesis and summarizes the importance

Essay Mentor Texts
Lower Level
The Pain and the Great One by Judy Blume
I Wanna Iguana by Karen Kaufman Orlof
Click, Clack, Moo: Cows That Type by Doreen Cronin

Upper Level
Hey World, Here I Am by Jean Little
The Down-to-Earth Guide To Global Warming by Laurie David, Cambria Gordon
Oh, Rats! The Story Of Rats And People by Marrin Albert

Learning Point
1. Know, understand, and apply features of an essay to make meaning as a reader and convey meaning as a writer.

5. Directions

Features of Directions

Why do we write directions?
- To explain how to go from one place to another

What are directions?
- Narrative or non-narrative description-explanation texts on how to go from one place to another in a sequence-time order

Forms and features of directions:
- Travel guide
- Pamphlet, brochure, hand-written note
- Map
- Numbered steps
- Diagrams and symbols

Directors Mentor Texts

Lower Level
Maisy Cleans Up by Lucy Cousins
This Is New York by Miroslav Sasek
The Raft by Jim LaMarche

Upper Level
Shortcut by David MacCaulay
Two Bad Ants by Chris Van Allsburg
Go Out and Play! by Darrell Hammond

Learning Point
1. Know, understand, and apply features of directions to make meaning as a reader and convey meaning as a writer.

6. Instructions

Features of Instructions

Why do we write instructions?
- To tell how to do something
- To tell how to operate a device

What are instructions?
- Narrative or non-narrative procedural texts that gives step-by-step actions to complete a task or operate a device

Forms and features of instructions:
- Owner's guide or how-to manual
- Numbers and steps
- Diagrams and figures

Instructions Mentor Texts

Lower Level
Angelo by David MacCaulay
The Way We Work by David MacCaulay
The New Way Things Work by David MacCaulay

Upper Level
Ship by David MacCaulay
Built to Last by David Macaulay
Underground by David Macaulay

Learning Point
1. Know, understand, and apply features of instructions to make meaning as a reader and convey meaning as a writer.

7. Realistic Fiction

Features of Realistic Fiction

Why do we write realistic fiction?
- To suggest probable events based upon modern characters, settings, and conflicts
- To encourage readers to experience modern events as though they were there
- To help readers gain perspective and empathy for the present based upon a probable story line

What is realistic fiction?
- A narrative work of fiction that presents scenarios according to what could happen in the real world

Forms and features of realistic fiction:
- Novel, short story, picture book, graphic novel, comic strip
- Characters, setting, conflict, resolution, and plot based on the current world situations
- Various modern world settings

Realistic Fiction Mentor Texts

Lower Level
Gooney Bird Greene by Lois Lowry
In Aunt Lucy's Kitchen by Cynthia Rylant
Fly Away Home by Eve Bunting

Upper Level
Every Living Thing by Cynthia Rylant
Maniac Magee by Jerry Spinelli
The Tiger Rising by Kate DiCamillo

Learning Point
1. Know, understand, and apply features of realistic fiction to make meaning as a reader and express meaning as a writer.

8. Historical Fiction

Features of Historical Fiction

Why do we write historical fiction?
- To bring history to life
- To encourage the reader to experience historical events as though they were there
- To help the reader understand the past

What is historical fiction?
- A narrative work of fiction that makes use of historical events, settings, and characters

Forms and features of historical fiction:
- Novel, short story, picture book, graphic novel, comic strip
- Characters, setting, conflict, resolution, and plot based on historical facts or probable situations
- Set in various places and times in history

Historical Fiction Mentor Texts
Lower Level
Small Wolf by Nathaniel Benchley
Will's Quill by Don Freeman
Dandelions by Eve Bunting

Upper Level
Role of Thunder, Hear My Cry by Mildred D. Taylor
Esperanza Rising by Pam Munoz Ryan
Bud, Not Buddy by Cristopher Paul Curtis

Learning Point
1. Know, understand, and apply features of historical fiction to make meaning as a reader and express meaning as a writer.

9. Science Fiction

Features of Science Fiction

Why do we write science fiction?
- To explore the possibilities of science and the worlds it might create
- To encourage the reader to see the world in a new and different way
- To entertain and provoke imagination

What is science fiction?
- Narrative work of fiction that makes use of scientific knowledge and speculation about what might be

Forms and features of science fiction:
- Novel short story, picture book, graphic novel, comic strip
- Plot based on scientific or technological speculation
- Set in a futuristic world, another world, or outer space

Science Fiction Mentor Texts

Lower Level
Wanna Buy an Alien by Eve Bunting
On the Dog by Judith Greenburg
Harriet's Hare by Dick King-Smith

Upper Level
Lion Boy by Zizou Corder
The City of Ember by Jeanne DuPrau
A Wrinkle in Time by Madeleine L'Engle

Learning Point
1. Know, understand, and apply features of science fiction to make meaning as a reader and express meaning as a writer.

10. Fantasy

Features of Fantasy

Why do we write fantasy?
- To take the reader into an imaginary world
- To explore the limits of human imagination

What is fantasy?
- Narrative work of fiction that does not reflect reality

Forms and features of fantasy:
- Novel, short story, picture book, graphic novel
- Strange events and behavior
- Detailed descriptions

Fantasy Mentor Texts

Lower Level
Where the Wild Things Are by Maurice Sendak
Jumanji by Chris Van Allsburg
Charlie and the Chocolate Factory by Roald Dahl

Upper Level
The Lion, the Witch, and the Wardrobe by C.S. Lewis
Phantom Tollbooth by Norton Juster
The Giver by Lois Lowry

Learning Point
1. Know, understand, and apply features of fantasy to make meaning as a reader and express meaning as a writer.

11. Fables and Fairy Tales

Features of Fables and Fairy Tales

Why do we write fables and fairy tales?
- To communicate and demonstrate a moral

What is a fable?
- Narrative work of fiction
- A short story, typically with animals as characters, conveying a moral

What is a fairy tale?
- Narrative work of fiction
- A short story with a message about life, typically with folkloric or fantasy characters, such as fairies, elves, giants, dwarves, and usually with magic

Forms and features of fables and fairy tales:
- Novel, short story, picture book, graphic novel
- The climax of the story is an element of trickery
- Emphasis on a moral or message about life

Fable and Fairy Tale Mentor Texts

Lower Level
A Twist in the Tail by Mary Hoffman
Fables by Arnold Lobel
Rumpelstiltskin by Paul O. Zelinsky

Upper Level
The Talking Eggs by Robert D. San Souci
Big Men, Big Country by Paul Robert Walker
Aesop's Fables by Jerry Pinkney

Learning Point
1. Know, understand, and apply features of fables and fairy tales to make meaning as a reader and express meaning as a writer.

12. Mystery

Features of Mystery

Why do we write mysteries?
- To experience suspense and solve mysterious situations

What is a mystery?
- Narrative work of fiction
- A story with a plot that involves a crime or other event that remains unsettled, a puzzle that needs to be solved until the very end

Forms and features of mysteries:
- Novel, short story, play
- Crimes
- Questions and clues
- Surprise ending
- Detectives

Mystery Mentor Texts

Lower Level
Nate the Great by Marjorie Sharmat
Cam Jansen and the Secret Service Mystery by David Alder
The Absent Author by Ron Roy

Upper Level
Things Hoped For by Andrew Clements
Chasing Vermeer by Blue Balliett
Scat by Carl Hiaasen

Learning Point
1. Know, understand, and apply features of mystery to make meaning as a reader and express meaning as a writer.

13. Myth

Features of a Myth

Why do we write myths?
- To explain how a person, place, or something came to exist
- To explain life, culture, and nature

What is a myth?
- Narrative work of fiction that explains the origins of life or the elements of nature
- A story containing a deeper truth and message about life
- A story that involves supernatural beings

Forms and features of myths:
- Novel, short story, picture book
- Characters are supernatural beings or elements of nature
- Explanation for the creation of something, which is often an element of nature
- Preserved through oral tradition in earlier times
- Collections of myths contribute to a culture

Myth Mentor Texts

Lower Level
The Children's Book of Myths and Legends by Ronne Randall
Persephone and the Pomegranate: A Myth from Greece by Kris Waldherr
The Arabian Nights by Neil Philip

Upper Level
D'Aulaires' Book of Greek Myths by Ingri d'Aulaire
American Indian Myths and Legends by Alfonso Ortiz
Tales from China by Cyril Birch

Learning Point
1. Know, understand, and apply features of myth to make meaning as a reader and express meaning as a writer.

14. Horror

Features of Horror

Why do we write horror?
- To evoke a feeling of dread in both the characters of the story and the reader

What is a horror?
- Narrative work of fiction that presents horror
- A story line of subtle anxiety to an intense feeling of fear, shock, or disgust

Forms and features of horror:
- Novel, short story, picture book, graphic novel
- Evil characters and elements
- Paranormal events
- Eerie and frightening atmosphere and setting
- Candor, teamwork, and chastity aid protagonists
- Evil characters or elements are not completely vanquished

Horror Mentor Texts

Lower Level
Para Norman: A Novel by Elizabeth Cody Kimmel
In a Dark, Dark Room and Other Scary Stories by Alvin Schwartz
Goosebumps Hall of Horrors #5: Don't Scream! by R.L. Stine

Upper Level
The Wolves in the Walls by Neil Gaiman
Coraline: The Graphic Novel by Neil Gaiman
Wait Till Helen Comes: A Ghost Story by Mary Downing Hahn

Learning Point
1. Know, understand, and apply features of horror to make meaning as a reader and express meaning as a writer.

Pillars
of Literacy

Writing

phases of
the writing process

five phases of
the writing process

---

phases of the writing process

Writers know writing is a process that has multiple steps and takes time. They do not just sit down, write a story, and that's it — done and perfect. Writers prewrite, draft, revise, edit, and publish.

Writers plan by prewriting, then write drafts and revise their drafts reflecting upon how they can improve their writing until they feel their work is fully developed. Writers do not focus on getting a personal narrative, story, report, or essay finished; they enjoy the process of writing by thoughtfully choosing words and crafting phrases, sentences, and passages that are original and theirs alone.

The writing process, keeping traits of writing in mind, is an effective way to express thoughts and ideas.

phases of the writing process

phases of the writing process

1. **Prewrite**
   Prewrite to prepare to draft. Develop seed ideas to reference. Produce a plot line for narrative writing or an outline for non-narrative writing. Gather and list ideas and details to support the plot line or outline.

2. **Draft**
   Draft sentences and passages to express ideas and thoughts. Write without too much concern for spelling and other conventions.   Work from prewriting to draft a rough version of a personal narrative, story, report, or essay.

3. **Revise**
   Revise to improve the quality of writing.   Reread drafts, both silently and aloud, to evaluate a piece of writing for its qualities and traits.

4. **Edit**
   Edit the conventions of writing.   Correct all errors.   Ask a writing partner to check conventions. (We develop a blind eye to our own work after re-reading it so many times!)

5. **Publish**
   Produce a final copy when the writing is fully developed and it is error-free. Use visual literacy, including text forms and features, to enhance meaning.

phases of the writing process

five phases of the writing process

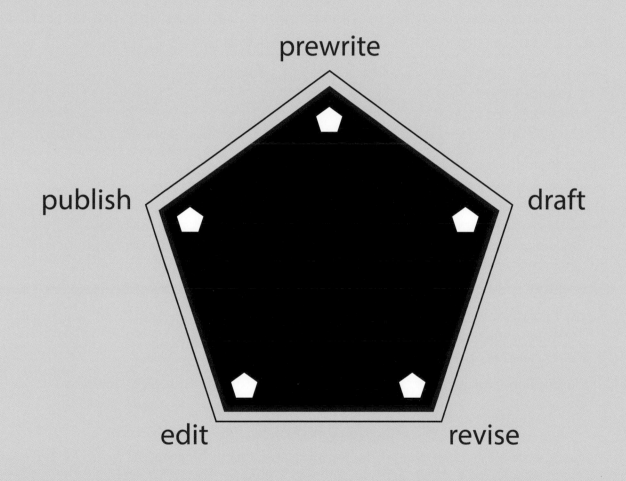

prewrite

publish

draft

edit

revise

1. Prewrite

Prewrite to prepare to draft. Develop seed ideas to work from. Produce a plot line for narrative writing or an outline for non-narrative writing. Gather and list ideas and details to support the plot line or outline.

Generating Seed Ideas (ideas for a story or subject)
> Generate lists of ideas
> Write out seed ideas
> Develop and grow seed ideas to use for a personal narrative, story, report, or essay

Story (narrative)
> Develop a story line: who did what, and why, with a conflict
> Determine the message of the story
> List the main character's desires and struggles, motivations, and challenges
> Develop the character sketch, the internal personality traits and external physical traits
> Sequence small moment scene seed ideas across a plot line or story mountain:
Exposition to Rising Action to Climax to Falling Action to Resolution

Report (non-narrative)
> Define the subject and central purpose, narrow the topic
> Determine the appropriate text structures to use:

description-explanation   sequence-time   problem-solution
persuasive   cause-effect   compare-contrast
> List main ideas to support the subject, draft topic sentences
> List details to support each topic sentence:
facts, examples, evidence, anecdotal stories, and notice-think-realize
> Determine a conclusion that leaves the reader thinking
> Sequence a boxes and bullets outline:
subject and introduction to main ideas and supporting details to conclusion

Essay (non-narrative)
> Define a thesis: a position to support or defend
> List main ideas to support the thesis and draft topic sentences
> List details to support each topic sentence:
facts, examples, evidence, anecdotal stories, and notice/think/realize
> Determine a conclusion that restates the thesis and challenges the reader to think
> Sequence a boxes and bullets outline:
introduction/thesis to topic sentences/supporting details to conclusion

phases of the writing process
prewrite

Enduring Understanding

Think About It. Talk About It.
Prewriting improves writing fluency.

Essential Question

Ask It. Answer It.
Why do we prewrite?

Learning Point
1. Writers get ready to draft by prewriting. They produce a seed idea and stretch it to develop a story line, subject, or position.
2. Writers develop a plot line or outline to follow to draft.
3. Writers gather and list ideas and details to support the plot line or outline.

2. Draft

Draft sentences and passages to express ideas and thoughts. Write without too much concern for spelling and other conventions. Work from prewriting to draft a rough version of a personal narrative, story, report, or essay.

Story
Draft small moment scenes across a plot line:
> exposition
> rising action
> climax
> falling action
> resolution

Report
Draft paragraphs across an outline for the introduction, main ideas and supporting details, and conclusion:
> introduction (subject)
> main idea
 - supporting details
> main idea
 - supporting details
> main idea
 - supporting details
> conclusion

Essay
Draft paragraphs across an outline for the introduction, topic sentences and supporting details, and conclusion:
> introduction (thesis)
> main idea
 - supporting details
> main idea
 - supporting details
> main idea
 - supporting details
> conclusion

phases of
the writing process

draft

Enduring Understanding

Think About It. Talk About It.
Drafting fluently enables expression of thoughts and ideas.

Essential Question

Ask It. Answer It.
Why do we draft?

Learning Points
1. Writers draft fluently, allowing thoughts and ideas to flow without concern for what might be good or bad, right or wrong, or for conventions.
2. Writers often begin two or three drafts and then decide which one to grow.

3. Revise

Revise to improve the quality of writing. Reread drafts, both silently and aloud, to evaluate a piece of writing for its qualities and traits.

Traits of Writing

1. Add more ideas and details. Delete unnecessary words.
2. Improve organization with better leads, sequences, transitions, and endings.
3. Further develop voice with an original way of saying things, showing energy and emotion.
4. Be sure word choice is accurate and precise so that it clearly conveys meaning.
5. Check sentence fluency so that the writing flows and is easy to read with a natural cadence and rhythm.

Small Moment Scene

Writing a personal narrative or story, we revise to improve small moment scenes, aiming to paint movies in the mind of the reader. We revise to improve how we show, not tell the setting, action, thoughts and feelings, and dialogue.

Notice, Think, Realize

Writing reports and essays, we revise to improve how we express what we notice, think, and realize. We revise to improve how we see more, hear more, smell more, taste more, and feel more in the world around us.

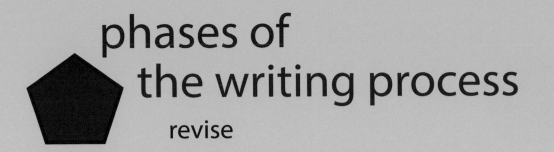

Enduring Understanding

Think About It. Talk About It.
Revising raises the quality of writing.

Essential Question

Ask It. Answer It.
Why do we revise?

Learning Points
1. Writers revise to improve a draft, focusing on the qualities and traits of writing.
2. Writers revise narrative writing by improving small moment scenes.
3. Writers revise non-narrative writing, improving how they express what they notice, think, and realize.

4. Edit

Edit the conventions of writing.   Correct all errors.   Ask a writing partner to check conventions. (We develop a blind eye to our own work after re-reading it so many times!)

Editing Marks

≡   Capitalize a letter

∕   Make a capital a lowercase letter

⊙   Add a period

⟍⟋   Take something out; delete

∧   Insert a word or letter

⩑   Insert punctuation

ⱽ   Insert apostrophe/quotation marks

◯ᵖ   Correct the spelling error

¶   Start a new paragraph

Sample of an Edited Passage

Max, who never liked touching slimy things, reachd down and grab the salamder I got it proclaimed max. He was so excitd about catching the Amphibian he did not worry about how it mite feel as they walked home, we talked about showing their catch to their friends. they decided to invite everyone to maxs house to see the specieman

(editor's marks in margins: e, bed, sp, lc salamander, that, might, they, specimen)

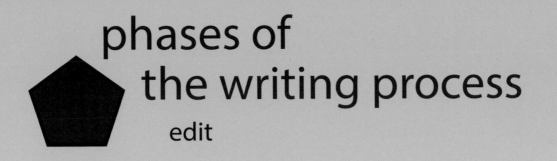

phases of the writing process

edit

Enduring Understanding

Think About It. Talk About It.
Editing produces error-free writing.

Essential Question

Ask It. Answer It.
Why do we edit?

Learning Point
1. Writers edit their writing, focusing on one convention at a time:
   spelling, capitalization, punctuation, or grammar.

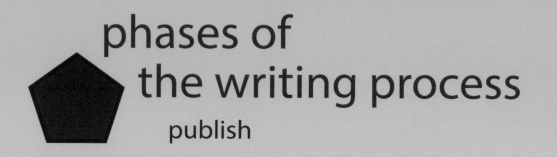

5. Publish

Produce a final copy when the writing is fully developed and it is error-free. Use visual literacy, including text forms and features, to enhance meaning.

Text Form
Determine what text form to use to publish the piece of writing.
(short story, novel, graphic novel, etc.)

Text Features
Determine the most effective use and design of text features to match the text form.
Determine the use and arrangement of text features to convey meaning.
(headings, subheadings, captions, illustrations, charts, graphs, maps, and fonts, etc.)

phases of the writing process
publish

Enduring Understanding

Think About It. Talk About It.
Publishing with text forms and features enhances meaning.

Essential Question

Ask It. Answer It.
Why do we publish?

Learning Point
1. Writers publish work focusing on visual literacy, including text forms and features.

Text Features - Print

Print	
Feature	**Helps learners...**
Acknowledgements	know an author's statement of indebtedness to others
Dedication	know who the author has dedicated the book to
Table of Contents	know key topics in a book and the order of presentation
Preface	get an overview of the content and a purpose for reading
Glossary	define important words contained in the text
Index	see content listed alphabetically with page numbers
Pronunciation Guide	to say the words correctly
Appendix	gain additional information at the end of a book
About the Author	gain background information about the author

Text Features - Illustrations

Illustrations	
Feature	**Helps learners...**
Photos	understand exactly what something looks like
Drawing	understand what something could or might look like
Magnification	see details in something small
Caricature	understand through exaggerated features
Portrait	view a realistic representation of a person
Book Jacket	gain a sense of the purpose and/or content of the book
Fashion Drawing	view a sleek style of a model, high fashion, or couture
Editorial Drawing	understand an editorial article in a publication
Medical Drawing	view medical products to physical anatomy

Text Features - Oganizational Aids

Organizational Aids	
Feature	**Helps learners...**
Bold Print	by signaling a word is important or found in the glossary
Italics / Colored Print	understand the word is important
Bullets	by emphasizing key points and concepts
Titles	locate different categories in the text
Headings	identify topics throughout the text as they skim and scan
Subheadings	navigate through sections of text
Captions	understand a picture or photograph
Labels	identify a picture or photograph and/or its parts
Sidebars	gather additional or explanatory information

Text Features - Graphic Aids

Graphic Aids	
Feature	**Helps learners...**
Diagrams	understand a detailed or simplified view of information
Flow Diagrams	understand a sequence of movements or actions
Comparison	understand one thing by comparing it to something else
Graphs	understand relativity between elements
Figures	combine text information with graphical aids
Maps	understand where things are in the world
Charts / Tables	summarize and/or compare information
Cross Sections	understand something by looking at it from the inside
Timelines	understand the sequence of events across time

phases of the writing process

story writing flowchart

Prewriting

> Seed Ideas

> Message

> Storyline

> Desires/Struggles

> Character Sketch

> Outline Plot

> Small Moments

Drafting

> Beginning, Middle, and End — the Plot

- Exposition
  introduction of the characters, setting, and background information - including an effective lead
- Rising Action
  the dialogue and action that present an unfolding conflict
- Climax
  the high point or turning point of action in the story
- Falling Action
  the dialogue and action that lead to the story's end
- Resolution
  the solution to the conflict and a satisfying end to the story

> Transition Words and Phrases

- At first > Soon > Suddenly > In the end

> Ending

- Make a point, reflect upon a character, or focus on a feeling

Revising

> Re-read and Improve

- Ideas
- Organization
- Voice
- Word Choice
- Sentence Fluency
- Small Moment Scenes

Editing

> Correct Conventions

- Spelling, Punctuation, Capitalization, and Grammar

Publishing

> Produce Final Copy

- Visual Literacy, Text Forms and Features

phases of
the writing process
information writing flowchart

Prewriting

> Seed Ideas

> Subject or Thesis

> Main Ideas/Topic Sentence

> Supporting Details

> Conclusion

> Notice/Think/Realize

> Text Structure
  - Description-Explanation
  - Sequence-Time
  - Problem-Solution
  - Persuasive
  - Cause-Effect
  - Compare-Contrast

Drafting

> Boxes and Bullets Outline
  - Introduction
    introduction of the subject with a thesis statement and background information
  - Main ideas and Topic Sentences
    the main ideas that support the subject or thesis
  - Supporting Details
    important details that support each main idea
  - Conclusion
    restatement of the subject or thesis, make a point, or raise an essential question

> Transition Words and Phrases
  - First > Equally important > Further > In conclusion

> Conclusion
  - Restate subject or thesis
  - Close with a question to ponder

Revising

> Re-read and Improve
- Ideas
- Organization
- Voice
- Word Choice
- Sentence Fluency
- Notice, Think, Realize

Editing

> Correct Conventions
  - Spelling, Punctuation, Capitalization, and Grammar

Publishing

> Produce Final Copy
  - Visual Literacy, Text Forms and Features

Pillars of Literacy

Presentation

traits of
presentation

traits of presentation

We might think that it takes a special kind of person to be able to make a presentation, read aloud to entertain, or perform in a play. Nonsense. What it takes is being able to understand and apply the Traits of Presentation.

Practice is key. We focus on our volume and clarity. We aim to speak so that the audience can hear and clearly understand. We engage the audience with our fluency, expression, and pace – speaking smoothly and naturally, with emotion and energy, and with varied pace, even pausing in silence from time to time for effect. We use body language and eye contact in order to bond with the audience, using body and hand movement to illustrate points and ideas. We use direct eye contact to connect with our listeners. We make time for preparation and rehearsal; we plan in advance and practice.

When we present to entertain, our purpose is to delight the audience – whether it is for humor, suspense, or wonder.

When we present to inform, our purpose is to educate or persuade the audience with information.

Whether presenting to entertain or inform, we engage the audience.

traits of presentation

four traits of presentation

traits of presentation

1. **Volume and Clarity**
   Speak with volume and clarity so that everyone in the audience can hear and understand.

2. **Fluency, Expression, and Pace**
   Speak smoothly, show emotion and energy, and vary the rate of speech for effect.

3. **Body Language and Eye Contact**
   Use hand and body movement for effect. Look directly at the audience.

4. **Preparation and Rehearsal**
   Plan in advance. Prepare and rehearse for a presentation. Practice.

traits of presentation

four traits of presentation

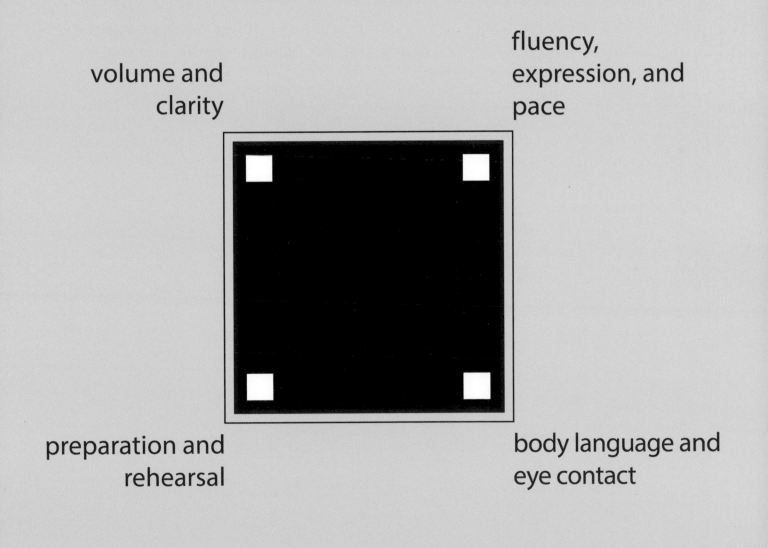

volume and
clarity

fluency,
expression, and
pace

preparation and
rehearsal

body language and
eye contact

1. Volume and Clarity

Speak with volume and clarity so that everyone in the audience can hear and understand. Speak slightly louder and more slowly than if engaged in a normal conversation with another person. Monitor volume and clarity throughout the presentation.

definition

volume
the appropriate loudness of voice

definition

clarity
the clearness of spoken or written language; the comprehensibility of clear expression; the enunciation of speech

traits of presentation

four traits of presentation

Enduring Understanding

Think About It. Talk About It.
Volume and clarity improves communiation and allows understanding.

Essential Question

Ask It. Answer It.
Why do we present with volume and clarity?

Learning Point
1. Presenters speak with an appropriate volume and clear enunciation.

2. Fluency, Expression, and Pace

Speak smoothly, show emotion and energy, and vary the rate of speech for effect. Speak naturally. Change the tone of voice to match the meaning of words. Vary the pace of speech by slowing down, speeding up, and pausing for effect.

definition

fluency
speaking or writing a language well; the ability to express oneself naturally by speaking smoothly and accurately

definition

expression
speaking with emotion and energy; the ability to express feelings and mood with tone of speech, facial expression, and body language

definition

pace
slowing down, speeding up, or pausing for effect when speaking or reading aloud

traits of presentation

four traits of presentation

Enduring Understanding

Think About It. Talk About It.
Fluency, expression, and pace enhance meaning.

Essential Question

Ask It. Answer It.
Why do we present with fluency, expression, and pace?

Learning Points
1. Presenters speak with fluency — smoothly and accurately.
2. Presenters speak with expression — communicating emotion and energy.
3. Presenters speak with varied pace — slowing down, speeding up, and pausing for effect.

3. Body Language and Eye Contact

Use hand and body movement for effect. Look directly at the audience. Make use of body language to convey meaning. Use movement and hand gestures in unison with words to emphasize ideas and emotions. Remain motionless at times in order to refocus the audience and provide a moment to reflect.

Use eye contact to engage the audience. Look at a section or group with a fixed gaze for a few seconds, ending with a smile before moving to make eye contact with another section of the audience.

definition **body language**
the use of hand and body movement to communicate

definition **eye contact**
a direct look to engage the audience

traits of
presentation
four traits of presentation

Enduring Understanding

Think About It. Talk About It.
Body language emphasizes ideas, while eye contact holds attention.

Essential Question

Ask It. Answer It.
Why do we present with body language and eye contact?

Learning Points
1. Presenters use body language — hand and body movement to convey meaning.
2. Presenters use eye contact — direct looks to engage the audience.

4. Preparation and Rehearsal

Plan in advance. Prepare and rehearse for a presentation. Practice. Develop, gather, and organize resources to make the presentation, such as visual aids.

Know that there is no substitute for rehearsal. Rehearse by presenting to a friend or in front of a mirror. Practice! Practice projecting voice with volume and clarity, and with fluency, expression, and pace. Practice body movement and hand gestures.

definition **preparation**
the process of gathering and organizing everything needed for storytelling or making a speech; producing a speech in writing or on note cards; producing visual aids; timing a presentation so that the content to be delivered matches the time available

definition **rehearsal**
the process of practicing in preparation for a presentation or performance

traits of presentation

four traits of presentation

Enduring Understanding

Think About It. Talk About It.
Preparation and rehearsal produce confidence.

Essential Question

Ask It. Answer It.
Why do we prepare and rehearse for a presentation?

Learning Points
1. Presenters prepare in advance for a presentation by developing, gathering, and organizing resources.
2. Presenters rehearse for a presentation by practicing the Traits of Presentation.

graphic organizers and rubrics

formative assessments

fifteen graphic organizers and rubrics

graphic organizers and rubrics

Graphic organizers enable us to focus and direct our thinking and learning. Learning becomes explicit and intentional.

Graphic organizers provide a framework for learning, enabling us to build and shape understanding with a visual map or diagram. Graphic organizers are effective visual learning strategies.

Rubrics enable us to evaluate our growth against defined criteria for learning. Simply, a rubric presents:

> Explicit learning points
> Criteria to evaluate learning
> Scores earned based on criteria

Rubrics provide us a common language with shared understandings of what the learning points are and the quality of work expected.

Traits of Conversation Graphic Organizer

Be Respectful	Be Prepared
Be an Active Listener	Be Clear
Inquire and Probe	Show Comprehension
Check Understanding	Control Self

Traits of Conversation Rubric

Traits of Conversation	2 Proficient	1 Developing	Traits of Conversation	2 Proficient	1 Developing
Be Respectful	Be respectful of group members and their thinking. Encourage others to share their thinking. Disagree politely. Make every effort to act with integrity.	Lacks: > Being respectful > Being polite > Giving encouragement > Demonstrating integrity	Inquire and Probe	Investigate, examine, scrutinize, and analyze thoughts and ideas. Ask others to support their thinking with evidence. Paraphrase to confirm or suspend assumptions.	Lacks: > Asking probing questions > Investigating the thoughts and ideas of others > Requesting evidence > Seeking confirmation of assumptions
Be Prepared	Focus on the topic, activate background knowledge, make connections. Prepare for conversations about shared reading by generating questions, taking notes, and marking passages. Participate and contribute to the conversation.	Lacks: > Being on topic > Preparation > Participation	Show Comprehension	Apply and exercise cognitive processes and meta-cognition. Make meaning through the elements of story or information. Analyze the quality of writing.	Lacks: > Demonstrating cognitive processes > Exercising meta-cognition > Making meaning through the elements of story or information > Discussing the quality of writing per the Traits of Writing
Be an Active Listener	Look with sincerity to the person speaking. Listen to comments and respond by asking questions to understand another's thinking or to build upon what is said.	Lacks: > Eye contact > Asking questions > Building upon others comments	Check Understanding	Examine thinking and ask questions to extend understanding. Share thoughts when understanding changes. Confidently share when unsure or when understanding breaks down.	Lacks: > Monitoring understanding > Sharing when thinking changes > Confidence to share when unsure or when understanding breaks down
Be Clear	Comment with clarity and be precise. Seek the same from others. Ask and answer questions with complete, detailed thoughts. Support ideas with evidence.	Lacks: > Speaking with clarity > Precise statements > Complete, detailed statements > Support of ideas with evidence	Control Self	Listen without interrupting. Monitor air time (how much and how often). Use wait time to allow others to join in the conversation. Monitor volume and tone.	Lacks: > Control by interrupting > Control by taking too much air time > Control by not using wait time > Control of volume and tone.

Story Summary / Retell Graphic Organizer

(summarize / retell in sequence as numbered)

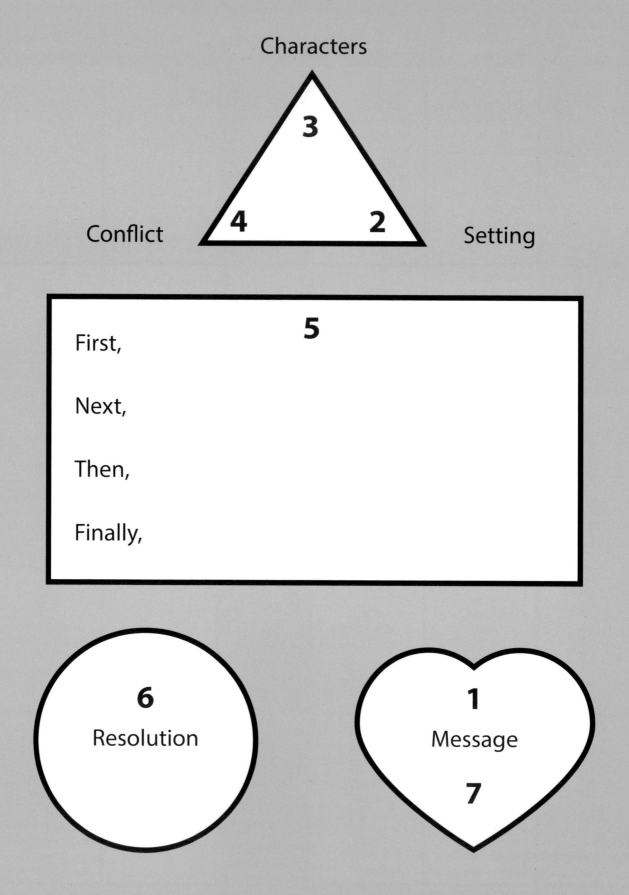

Characters

3

Conflict 4 2 Setting

5

First,

Next,

Then,

Finally,

6
Resolution

1
Message

7

168

Story Summary / Retell Rubric

Traits of Summary	4 Exemplary	3 Proficient	2 Developing	1 Beginning
Message and "Gist"	The summary or retelling includes a detailed explanation of the story's theme and the message or lesson to be learned.	The summary or retelling includes a general explanation of the story's theme and the message or lesson to be learned.	The summary or retelling includes an incomplete explanation of the story's theme and the message or lesson to be learned.	The summary or retelling is an inaccurate explanation of the story's theme and the message or lesson to be learned.
Story Elements (characters, setting, conflict, resolution, and events)	The summary or retelling contains detailed statements of all story elements and their connection to one another.	The summary or retelling contains general statements of most of the story elements and their connection to one another.	The summary or retelling contains incomplete statements of the story elements and their connection to one another.	The summary or retelling contains inaccurate or no restatement of the story elements.
Organization	Events are retold in a complete, logical sequence with a clear beginning, middle, and end. Transitions are used effectively.	Events are retold in a somewhat logical sequence with a beginning, middle, and end. Transitions are evident.	Events are retold in a somewhat disconnected fashion. The beginning, middle, and/or end may be incomplete or left out. Few, if any, transitions are used.	Events are retold but show no logical sequence.
Linguistic Spillover	Use of language indicates an elaborated and personalized understanding of the story. Voice and Word Choice are very much evident.	Use of language indicates a general understanding of the story. Voice and Word Choice are somewhat evident.	Use of language indicates a superficial understanding of the story. Voice and Word Choice are limited or not evident.	Use of language is limited and does not show an understanding of the story.

Chapter Summary / Retell Graphic Organizer

(summarize / retell in sequence as numbered)

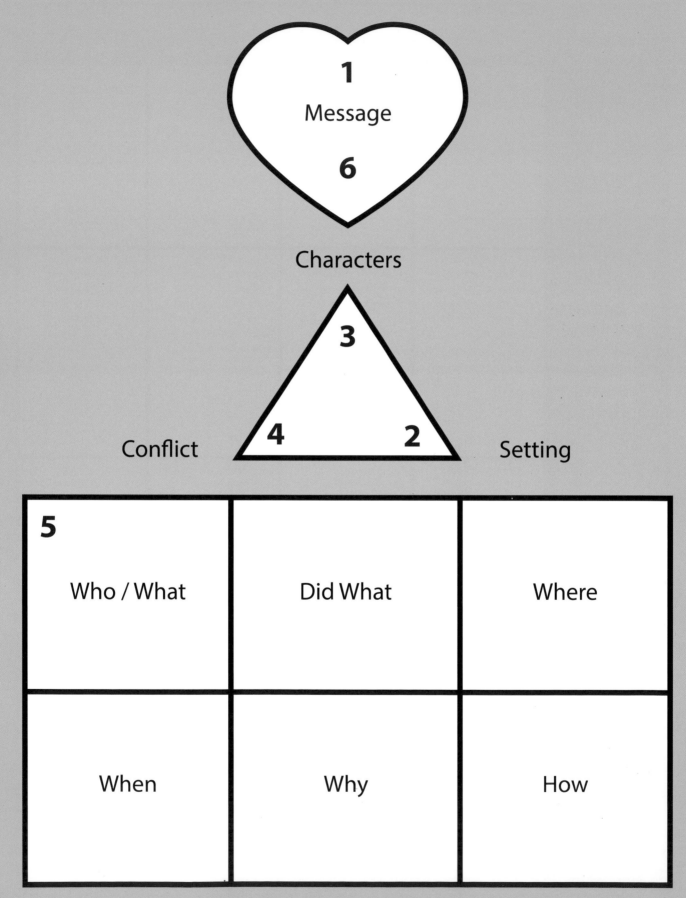

1
Message

6

Characters

3

Conflict **4**   **2** Setting

5 Who / What	Did What	Where
When	Why	How

Chapter Summary / Retell Rubric

Traits of Summary	4 Exemplary	3 Proficient	2 Developing	1 Beginning
Message and "Gist"	The summary or retelling includes a complete explanation that states the chapter's message, main idea, and/or event.	The summary or retelling includes a general explanation that states the chapter's message, main idea, and/or event.	The summary or retelling is an incomplete statement of the chapter's message, main idea, and/or event.	The summary or retelling indicates minimal understanding or no reference to the chapter's message, main idea, and/or event.
Story Elements (characters, setting, conflict, resolution, and events)	The summary or retelling contains complete, detailed statements of all story elements and their connection to one another relative to the chapter's message, main idea, and/or event.	The summary or retelling contains general statements of most of the story elements and their connection to one another relative to the chapter's message, main idea, and/or event.	The summary or retelling contains incomplete statements of the story elements and their connection to one another relative to the chapter's message, main idea, and/or event.	The summary or retelling contains inaccurate statements or no statement of story elements.
Organization	Events are retold following a logical sequence with a beginning, middle, and end, including a focus on who did what, where, when, why, and how. Transitions are used effectively.	Events are retold in a somewhat logical sequence with a beginning, middle, and end, with some aspects of who did what, where, when, why, and how. Transitions are evident.	Events are retold in a somewhat disconnected fashion. The beginning, middle, and/or end may be incomplete or left out. Few, if any, transitions are used.	Events are retold but show no logical sequence.
Linguistic Spillover	Use of language indicates an elaborated and personalized understanding of the chapter. Voice and Word Choice are very much evident.	Use of language indicates a general understanding of the chapter. Voice and Word Choice are somewhat evident.	Use of language indicates a superficial understanding of the chapter. Voice and Word Choice are limited or not evident.	Use of language is incorrect or limited and does not show an understanding of the chapter.

Information Summary Graphic Organizer

(summarize / retell in sequence as numbered)

1

Subject and Central Purpose

2

Who / What	Did What	Where
When	Why	How

3

Notice, Think, Realize

Information Summary Rubric

Traits of Summary	4 Exemplary	3 Proficient	2 Developing	1 Beginning
Subject and Central Purpose **"Gist"**	The summary includes a complete, detailed explanation of the subject and central purpose of the selection.	The summary includes a general explanation of the subject and central purpose of the selection.	The summary includes an incomplete explanation of the subject and central purpose of the selection.	The summary is an inaccurate explanation of the subject and central purpose of the selection.
Main Ideas and Supporting Details	The summary contains clear and detailed statements of the main ideas and important supporting details.	The summary contains general statements of the main ideas and some important supporting details.	The summary contains incomplete statements of the main ideas and important supporting details.	The summary contains inaccurate or no statements of the main ideas and important supporting details.
Notice, Think, Realize	The conclusion contains meaningful and insightful details about what is noticed, thought about, and realized.	The conclusion contains some details about what is noticed, thought about, and realized.	The conclusion contains few details about what is noticed, thought about, and realized.	The conclusion contains inaccurate or no details about what is noticed, thought about, and realized.
Organization	Events are retold following a logical, well sequenced introduction (subject and central purpose), body (who did what, where, when, why, and how), and conclusion (notice, think, and realize).	Events are retold following a somewhat logical sequence with an introduction (subject and central purpose), body (who did what, where, when, why, and how), and conclusion (notice, think, and realize).	Events are retold following an incomplete or inaccurate sequence, without a clear introduction, body, and conclusion. The specifics of who did what, where, when, why, and how are lacking.	Few or no events are retold.
Linguistic Spillover	Use of technical language indicates a significant expanding oral language capacity and understanding of the information. Voice and Word Choice are very much evident.	Use of technical language indicates a somewhat expanding oral language capacity and understanding of the information. Voice and Word Choice are evident.	Use of technical language indicates little expanding oral language capacity and understanding of the information. Voice and Word Choice are weak.	Use of technical language is incorrect or limited and does not show a growing oral language capacity.

Cognitive Processes Graphic Organizer

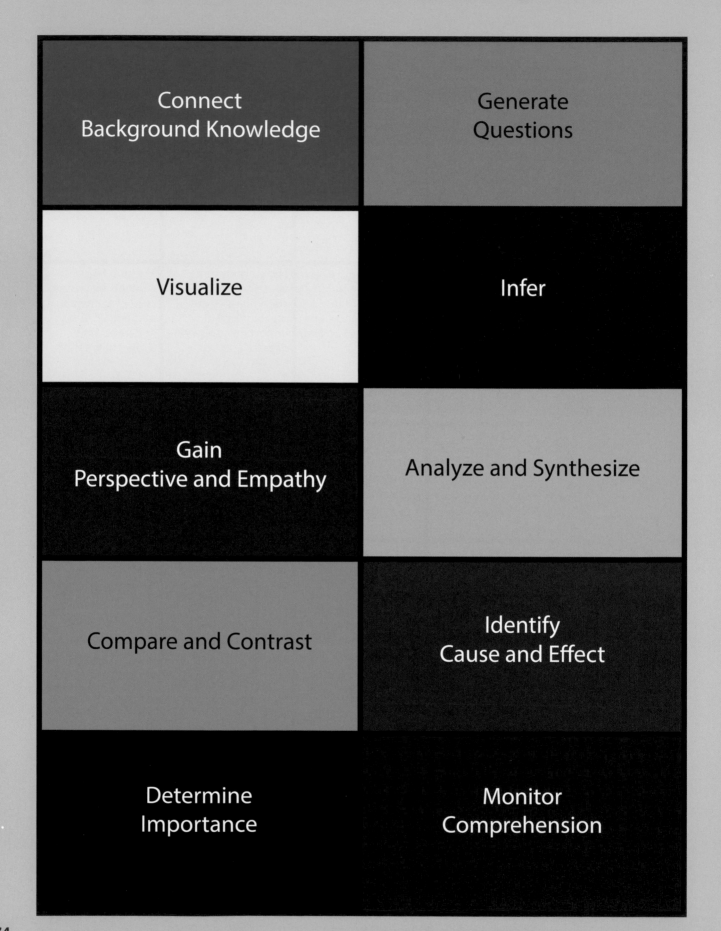

Connect
Background Knowledge

Generate
Questions

Visualize

Infer

Gain
Perspective and Empathy

Analyze and Synthesize

Compare and Contrast

Identify
Cause and Effect

Determine
Importance

Monitor
Comprehension

Cognitive Processes Rubric

Cognitive Processes	2 Proficient	1 Developing	Cognitive Processes	2 Proficient	1 Developing
Connect Background Knowledge	Makes multiple, detailed connections to background knowledge and/or personal experience.	Makes few or no connections to background knowledge and/or personal experience.	Analyze and Synthesize	Understands by taking apart the constitution or structure of something. Understands by putting pieces of knowledge together.	Unable to take apart the constitution or structure of something. Unable to put pieces of knowledge together.
Generate Questions	Asks multiple open-ended questions to extend thinking and/or propel reading forward.	Asks few or no open-ended questions.	Compare and Contrast	Identifies and thinks about similarities and differences.	Unable to identify similarities and differences.
Visualize	Forms multiple mental sensory and emotional images to make meaning.	Forms few or no mental sensory and emotional images.	Identify Cause and Effect	Determines why events happen and the resulting effect.	Unable to determine why events happen or the resulting effect.
Infer	Determines what is implied, supported by evidence and connections: text-to-text, text-to-self, and text-to-world.	Unable to determine what is implied or to support thinking with evidence.	Determine Importance	Determines important ideas and details to build and shape understanding.	Unable to determine important ideas and details to build and shape understanding.
Gain Perspective and Empathy	Understands the viewpoint of the character and the character's emotions.	Unable to understand the viewpoint of the character or the character's emotions.	Monitor Comprehension	Recognizes when understanding breaks down or changes, and asks questions.	Unable to recognize when understanding breaks down or changes, and fails to ask questions.

Character Analysis Graphic Organizer

Why did the character act this way? Interpretation	Was it right or wrong for the character to act this way? Reflection	What did the character get from acting this way? Interpretation
How am I like the character in this story? Reflection	What is the lesson learned? Reflection	How has this lesson changed the way I think? Reflection

Character Analysis Rubric

Traits of Character Analysis	4 Exemplary	3 Proficient	2 Developing	1 Beginning
Why did the character act this way? INTERPRETATION	A detailed account of why the character did what he or she did, supported by evidence from the text and the character traits implied.	A general account of why the character did what he or she did, partially supported by evidence from the text.	A limited account of why the character did what he or she did, supported by little or no evidence from the text.	An inaccurate account or no account of why the character did what he or she did, with no evidence from the text.
Was it right or wrong for the character to act this way? REFLECTION	A detailed explanation reflecting whether it was right or wrong for the character to act this way, supported by evidence from the text/background knowledge.	A general explanation reflecting whether it was right or wrong for the character to act this way, partially supported by evidence from the text/background knowledge.	An limited explanation reflecting whether it was right or wrong for the character to act this way, supported by little or no evidence.	An inaccurate explanation or no explanation of whether it was right or wrong for the character to act this way.
What did the character get by acting this way? INTERPRETATION	A detailed explanation of what the character got by acting this way, supported by evidence from the text and character traits implied.	A general explanation of what the character got by acting this way, partially supported by evidence from the text.	A limited explanation of what the character got from acting this way, supported by little or no evidence from the text.	An inaccurate explanation or no explanation of what the character got from acting this way.
How am I like the character in this story? REFLECTION	A detailed explanation reflecting how you see yourself as the same or different from the character, supported by evidence from the text/background knowledge.	A general explanation reflecting how you see yourself as the same or different from the character, supported by some evidence from the text/background knowledge.	A limited explanation reflecting how you see yourself as the same or different from the character, supported by little evidence from the text/background knowledge.	An inaccurate explanation or no explanation reflecting how you see yourself as the same or different from the character.
What is the lesson learned? REFLECTION	A detailed explanation of the lesson learned, supported by evidence from the text/background knowledge.	A general explanation of the lesson learned, partially supported by evidence from the text/background knowledge.	A limited explanation of the lesson learned, supported by little or no evidence.	An inaccurate explanation or no explanation of the lesson learned.
How has this lesson changed the way I think? REFLECTION	A detailed explanation reflecting how the lesson learned changes the way you think, supported by evidence from the text/background knowledge.	A general explanation reflecting how the lesson learned changes the way you think, supported by limited evidence from the text/background knowledge.	A limited explanation reflecting how the lesson learned changes the way you think, supported by little or no evidence from the text/background knowledge.	An inaccurate explanation or no explanation of how the lesson learned changes the way you think.

Character Traits Graphic Organizer

Character Traits
Attitudes and Attributes

Positive	Negative
accepts authority, loyal, devoted	rebellious
affectionate	ignores, cold, aloof
aspiring, ambitious, motivated, curious	lazy, apathetic, unmotivated
candid	closed, guarded, secretive
cheerful	cheerless, gloomy, sour, grumpy
considerate, thoughtful, compassionate	inconsiderate, thoughtless
cooperative	uncooperative, unhelpful, combative
courageous, brave, adventurous	cowardly, cowering, fearful
courteous, caring, polite, well-mannered	rude, impolite, uncaring, callous
creative, innovative, imaginative	indecisive, unsure
endures, perseveres	relents, gives up
enthusiastic	unenthusiastic, apathetic, indifferent
faith in life, oneself, others	life can't be trusted, lacks faith in self, unreliable
flexible	inflexible, rigid, unbending, stubborn
forgiving	unforgiving, resentful, spiteful
friendly	unfriendly, aloof, unsociable, hostile
frugal, thrifty	wasteful, spendthrift
generous	stingy, miserly, selfish

Character Traits Rubric

Character Traits
Attitudes and Attributes

Positive	Negative
graceful	clumsy
goodwill	ill-will, malice, selfish
humble, modest	arrogant, conceited
insightful	lacks insight, blind to, ignorant of
patient	impatient, expectant
punctual	late
resourceful	helpless
responsible	irresponsible
risk-taker	adverse to risk
stamina	lack of stamina, weak
stress-free, relaxed	stressed, tense
talented	untalented, limited, inept
tough	weak, soft, light, lenient
trustworthy, dependable, honest	untrustworthy, undependable, dishonest

Character Traits	4 Exemplary	3 Proficient	2 Developing	1 Beginning
Implied Character Traits	Identifies three or more character traits implied, supported with evidence.	Identifies one or two character traits implied, supported with evidence.	Identifies one character trait implied, partially supported with evidence.	Inaccurately identifies a character trait implied.

Main Idea Analysis Graphic Organizer

State a main idea and important supporting details.	How does this information connect with what we already know?	What are the cause and effect relationships?
Interpretation	Reflection	Interpretation
Why is this information important?	How will this information change the way we think?	What are the enduring understandings or essential questions?
Reflection	Interpretation	Reflection

Main Idea Analysis Rubric

Traits of Main Idea Analysis	4 Exemplary	3 Proficient	2 Developing	1 Beginning
Summarize a main idea and important supporting details. INTERPRETATION	A complete, detailed explanation of the main idea, including several important details as supporting evidence from the text.	A general explanation of the main idea, supported by a few pieces of evidence from the text.	A limited or partially inaccurate explanation of the main idea, supported by one piece of evidence or no evidence from the text.	An inaccurate explanation of the main idea without any supporting details from the text or no explanation at all.
How does this information connect with what we know? REFLECTION	A detailed reflection of what I notice, think, and realize about a main idea supported by background knowledge and personal experience.	A general reflection of what I notice, think, and realize about a main idea supported by some background knowledge or personal experience.	A limited reflection of what I notice, think, and realize about a main idea supported by little background knowledge or personal experience.	An inaccurate reflection or no reflection of what I notice, think, and realize about a main idea.
What are the cause and effect relationships? INTERPRETATION	A detailed explanation of why something happens and the resulting effect, supported by evidence from the text/background knowledge.	A general explanation of why something happens and the resulting effect, supported by evidence from the text/background knowledge.	A limited explanation of why something happens and the resulting effect, supported by little evidence.	An inaccurate explanation or no explanation of why something happens and the resulting effect.
Why is this information important? REFLECTION	A detailed reflection about how this information is important, supported by evidence from the text/background knowledge.	A general reflection about how this information is important, supported by some evidence from the text/background knowledge.	A limited reflection about how this information is important supported by little evidence.	An inaccurate reflection or no reflection about how this information is important.
How will this information change the way we think? INTERPRETATION	A detailed explanation of how this information might change the way people think, supported by evidence from the text/background knowledge.	A general explanation of how this information might change the way people think, supported by evidence from the text/background knowledge.	A limited explanation of how this information might change the way people think, supported by little or no evidence from the text/background knowledge.	A inaccurate explanation or no explanation of how this information might change the way people think.
What are the enduring understandings and essential questions? REFLECTION	A detailed reflection about the enduring understandings and essential questions that show the meaning and message of this information.	A general reflection about enduring understandings and essential questions that show the meaning or message of this information.	A limited reflection about enduring understandings and essential questions that show the meaning or message of this information.	An inaccurate reflection or no reflection about enduring understandings and essential questions.

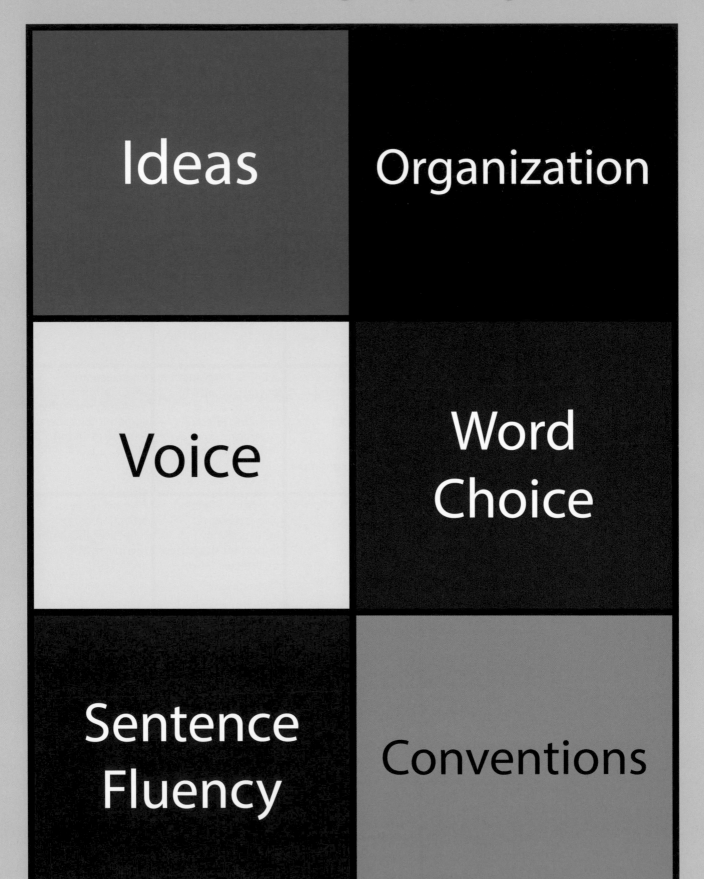

Ideas

Organization

Voice

Word Choice

Sentence Fluency

Conventions

Six Traits of Writing Rubric

Traits of Writing	5 Exemplary	3 Proficient	1 Beginning
Ideas	Rich ideas and details add meaning to the writing. A. Topic is narrow and manageable B. Ideas are crystal clear and supported with details C. Relevant details in support of the topic go beyond the obvious D. Ideas are fresh and original E. Insightful topic	Ideas are basic. Details support ideas. A. The topic is broad B. Reasonably clear ideas C. Support is attempted D. Difficulty going from general observations about topic to specifics	Ideas are not clear. There are sketchy or missing details. A. Still in search of a topic and main ideas B. Details support the main ideas, but are limited C. Topic is not clearly defined D. Topic may be repetitious, disconnected, and contains too many random thoughts
Organization	Organizational structure has a logical sequence with a beginning, middle, and end (narrative) or introduction, body, and conclusion (non-narrative). A. Inviting beginning or introduction draws the reader in; a satisfying ending or conclusion leaves the reader with a sense of closure B. Transitions connect ideas C. Sequencing is logical and effective D. Pacing is well controlled E. Text structure matches purpose, and paragraphing is strong	Organizational structure generally moves the reader through the text without confusion. A. Beginning or introduction is evident; conclusion is evident B. Transitions sometimes work C. Sequencing is present, yet structure takes attention away from content D. Pacing is sometimes controlled E. Organizational structure supports the story line or main point with an attempt at paragraphing	Organizational structure lacks a clear sense of direction. A. No real lead or conclusion B. Connections between ideas, if present, are confusing C. Sequencing needs work D. Pacing feels awkward E. Problems with text structure make it hard for the reader to get a grip on a main idea or story line. Little or no evidence of paragraphing is present
Voice	Writing has an original style and personal tone. There is a sense that a real person is behind the words. Writing shows emotion and energy. A. Figurative language strongly connects with the reader B. There are revealing details C. Narrative writing is honest, personal, and engaging D. Information or persuasive writing reflects commitment to topic	Writing seems sincere, but not fully engaged or involved. Writing is not compelling. A. Attempt to connect with audience is evident but impersonal B. Some revealing details C. Narrative writing reflects limited perspective D. Information or persuasive writing lacks consistent focus on the topic	Writing seems uninvolved with the topic and the audience. A. Fails to connect with audience B. Purpose is unclear C. Writing has no sense of the writer D. Narrative writing lacks a point of view E. Expository or persuasive shows no engagement with the topic
Word Choice	Accurate words convey precise meaning. A. Words are specific and accurate B. Striking words create imagery C. Precise nouns, descriptive adjectives, strong verbs, and illustrative adverbs are evident	Words are functional, but lack energy. A. Words are generally correct B. Attempts at colorful language C. Every day nouns, passive verbs, and mundane modifiers are used D. Language is unremarkable, with one or two fine moments	Words demonstrate a limited vocabulary. A. Words are nonspecific B. Many of the words don't work C. Language is used incorrectly D. Misused parts of speech E. Language is unimaginative
Sentence Fluency	Sentences have a natural rhythm and cadence. Writing is easy to read with expression and pace. A variety of sentence types flow together naturally. Sentences have a variety of beginnings and varied length. A. Sentences vary in length as well as structure B. Sentence beginnings are varied C. Writing has cadence	Writing has a steady beat, but tends to lack variety and a creative flow. A. Sentences are of a routine fashion B. Sentences are usually of similar length, yet constructed correctly C. Sentence beginnings are sometimes varied D. Parts of the text invite expressive oral reading, but other parts are stiff	Writing does not allow for fair expressive, interpretive reading. A. Sentences are choppy, incomplete, rambling, or awkward. B. Sentences begin the same way C. Writing does not invite expressive oral reading
Conventions	The conventions of writing are error-free: capitalization, punctuation, grammar, and spelling. A. Spelling is generally correct B. Punctuation is correct C. Capitalization is correct D. Grammar and usage are correct E. Paragraphing tends to be sound F. The writer may manipulate and/or edit for stylistic effect - and it works	The conventions of writing are partially error-free: capitalization, punctuation, grammar, and spelling. A. Spelling is usually correct B. End punctuation is usually correct C. Most capitalization is correct D. Problems with grammar and usage are not serious E. Paragraphing is attempted F. Editing is moderate, inconsistent	Errors in spelling, punctuation, capitalization, usage and grammar, and/or paragraphing make text difficult to read. A. Spelling errors are frequent B. Punctuation is missing, incorrect C. Capitalization is random D. Errors in grammar are common E. Paragraphing is missing F. Little, if any, editing

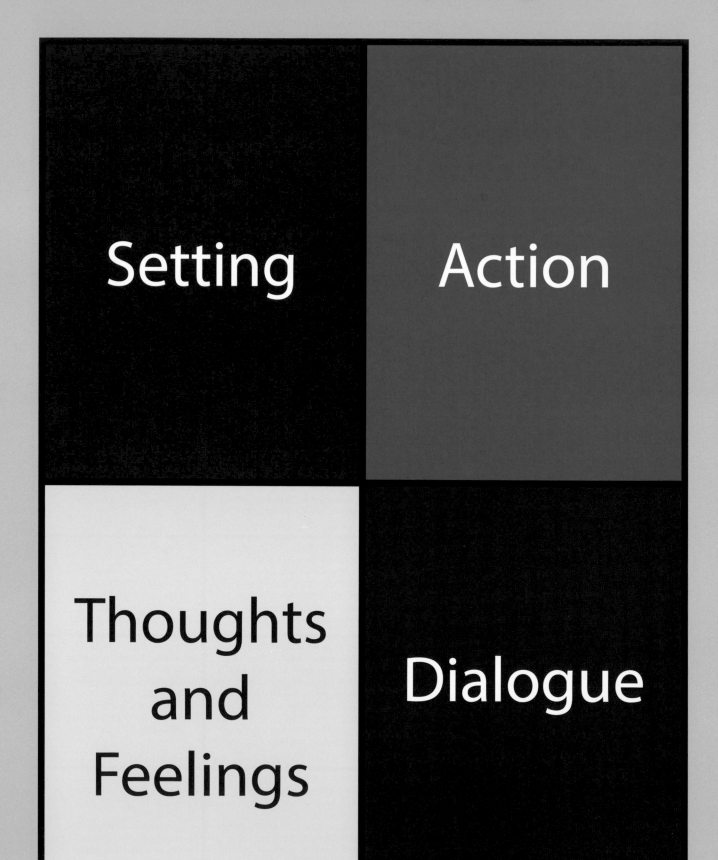

Setting

Action

Thoughts and Feelings

Dialogue

Small Moment Scene Rubric

Small Moment Scene	4 Exemplary	3 Proficient	2 Developing	1 Beginning
Setting	Shows vivid images of a location's physical details including the time of day, weather, and the attributes of objects such as light, color, texture, and sensory qualities like smell and touch.	Shows general images of a location's physical details including the time of day, weather, and the attributes of objects such as light, color, texture, and sensory qualities like smell and touch.	Tends to tell, rather than show. Shows few images of a location's physical details such as the time of day, weather, and the attributes of objects such as light, color, texture, or sensory qualities like smell and touch.	Tells or makes no mention of a location's physical details.
Action	Shows vivid images of a character's actions, including details of movement, the rate of the speed, and the emotion and energy behind the action.	Shows general images of a character's actions, including the details of movement, the rate of the speed, and the emotion and energy behind the action.	Tends to tell rather than show. Shows few images of a character's actions, or the details of movement, the rate of the speed, or the emotion and energy behind the action.	Tells or makes no mention of a character's actions.
Thoughts and Feelings	Shows many vivid and detailed images of how the character experienced their thoughts and feelings, using words such as: > wondered > thought > felt > realized > determined	Shows some images of how the character experienced their thoughts and feelings, using words such as: > wondered > thought > felt > realized > determined	Tends to tell, rather than show. Tells or shows few images of the how the character experienced their thoughts and feelings.	Tells or makes no mention of how the character experienced their thoughts and feelings.
Dialogue	Shows vivid and detailed images of how the character said what they said, using the conventions of dialogue and words such as: > declared > shouted > bellowed > whispered > suggested	Shows general images of how the character said what they said, using the conventions of dialogue and words such as: > declared > shouted > bellowed > whispered > suggested	Tends to tell, rather than show. Tells or shows few images of how the character said what they said, nor consistently uses the conventions of dialogue. Most often uses basic words to tell dialogue such as: > said > asked	Tells or makes no mention of what the character said. Does not use the conventions of dialogue.

Story Mountain Graphic Organizer

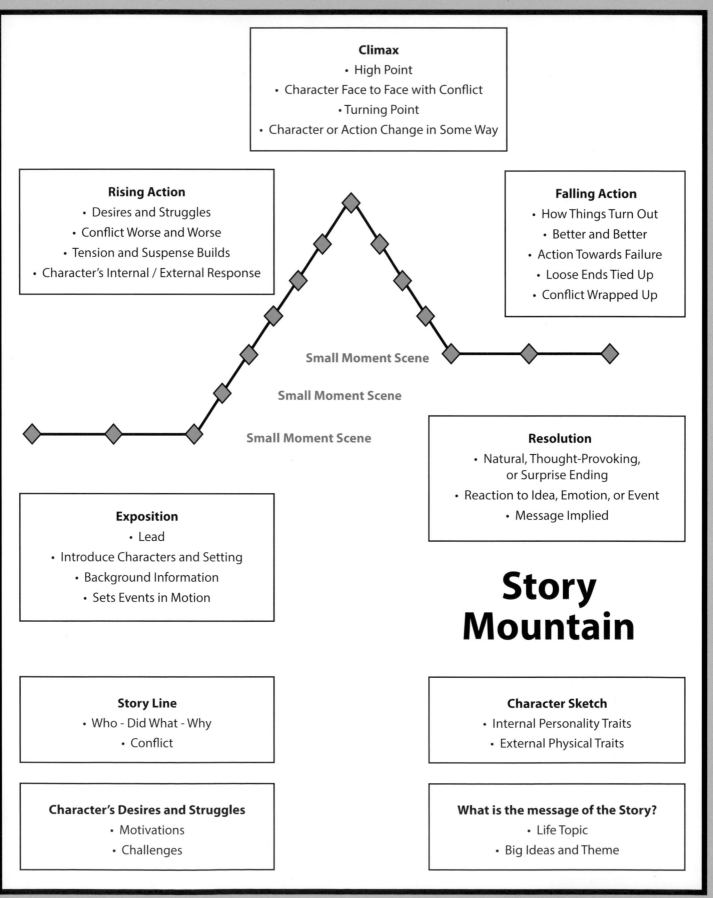

Climax
- High Point
- Character Face to Face with Conflict
- Turning Point
- Character or Action Change in Some Way

Rising Action
- Desires and Struggles
- Conflict Worse and Worse
- Tension and Suspense Builds
- Character's Internal / External Response

Falling Action
- How Things Turn Out
- Better and Better
- Action Towards Failure
- Loose Ends Tied Up
- Conflict Wrapped Up

Small Moment Scene

Small Moment Scene

Small Moment Scene

Exposition
- Lead
- Introduce Characters and Setting
- Background Information
- Sets Events in Motion

Resolution
- Natural, Thought-Provoking, or Surprise Ending
- Reaction to Idea, Emotion, or Event
- Message Implied

Story Mountain

Story Line
- Who - Did What - Why
- Conflict

Character Sketch
- Internal Personality Traits
- External Physical Traits

Character's Desires and Struggles
- Motivations
- Challenges

What is the message of the Story?
- Life Topic
- Big Ideas and Theme

Story Mountain Rubric

Story Mountain	4 Exemplary	3 Proficient	2 Developing	1 Beginning
Exposition	An engaging lead hooks the reader. The introduction of the characters and setting has depth. The story's conflict is hinted at or introduced. The story is set in motion.	The introduction of the characters and setting is evident. Some background information sets up the story.	The introduction of the characters and setting is limited. There is little or no background information to set up the story.	There is no sense of who the main characters are, the setting, or where the story is headed.
Rising Action	A gradual unfolding of the character's desires and struggles is clearly evident. The conflict becomes worse and worse. The tension or suspense builds. The character's traits are reflected in response to events.	There is some sense of an unfolding of the character's desires and struggles. The conflict is evident. The character's traits are sometimes reflected in response to events.	There is little sense of the character's desires and struggles. The conflict is not made clear. The character's traits are not reflected in response to events.	The character's desires and struggles are not evident. The conflict is not evident.
Climax	The character comes face to face with the conflict. There is clearly a turning point in the story, where the character and/or action changes in some way.	There is some sense that the conflict has played out and the climax has arrived. There is some sense that there is a turning point in the story.	There is little sense that conflict has played out or that there is a turning point in the story.	There is no sense that there is a climax or turning point in the story.
Falling Action	Following the turning point, it is evident that there is a progression towards the resolution; things become better and/or worse. Loose ends are tied up and the conflict is wrapped up.	There is some sense that there is a progression towards the resolution; things become better or worse.	There is a limited sense that there is a progression towards the resolution.	There is no progression towards the resolution.
Resolution	There is a natural, thought-provoking, or surprise ending. There is a reaction to an idea, emotion, or event. The message of the story is made explicit or implied.	There is a sense that the ending has arrived. The message of the story is somewhat conveyed.	There is little sense that the ending has arrived.	There is no sense that the ending has arrived. The reader is left hanging.

I notice...

I think...

I realize...

Notice, Think, Realize Rubric

Notice Think Realize	4 Exemplary	3 Proficient	2 Developing	1 Beginning
Notice	There is a clear sense that the writer notices details in the world around us. With insight, the writer sees more, hears more, smells more, tastes more, and feels more.	There is some sense that the writer notices details in the world around us. The writer sees more, hears more, smells more, tastes more, and feels more.	There is little sense that the writer notices more than what is obvious in world around us. The writer is still learning what it means to gain insights and see more, hear more, smell more, taste more, and feel more.	There is no indication that anything but the obvious is noticed.
Think	There Is a clear sense that what is noticed makes us think. Multiple types of cognitive processes and meta-cognition are exercised to express insights and understandings: > make connections > generate questions > visualize > infer > gain perspective and empathy > identify cause and effect > compare and contrast > analyze and synthesize > determine importance > monintor comprehension	There is some sense that what is noticed makes us think. Some cognitive processes and meta-cognition are exercised to express insights and understandings: > make connections > generate questions > visualize > infer > gain perspective and empathy > identify cause and effect > compare and contrast > analyze and synthesize > determine importance > monintor comprehension	There is little sense that what is noticed makes us think. Cognitive processes or meta-cognition is barely, if at all, used: > make connections > generate questions > visualize > infer > gain perspective and empathy > identify cause and effect > compare and contrast > analyze and synthesize > determine importance > monintor comprehension.	There is no indication that anything noticed is truly thought about.
Realize	There is a clear sense that what is noticed and thought about is reflected upon and connected to meaning, a message, and life's lessons.	There is some sense that what is noticed and thought about is reflected upon and connected to meaning, a message, and life's lessons.	There is little sense that what is noticed and thought about is reflected upon and connected to meaning, a message, and life's lessons.	There is no sense that what is noticed is thought about.

Boxes and Bullets Graphic Organizer

THESIS STATEMENT
Claim or Position

TOPIC SENTENCE
A Main Idea Showing the Claim or Position

SUPPORTING EVIDENCE AND THOUGHT
- Evidence, Facts
- Anecdotal Story
- I Notice, I Think, I Realize

TOPIC SENTENCE
A Main Idea Showing the Claim or Position

SUPPORTING EVIDENCE AND THOUGHT
- Evidence, Facts
- Anecdotal Story
- I Notice, I Think, I Realize

TOPIC SENTENCE
A Main Idea Showing the Claim or Position

SUPPORTING EVIDENCE AND THOUGHT
- Evidence, Facts
- Anecdotal Story
- I Notice, I Think, I Realize

Closing Statement
Restate Claim or Position

Boxes and Bullets Rubric

Boxes and Bullets	4 Exemplary	3 Proficient	2 Developing	1 Beginning
Thesis Statement and Introduction	A strong thesis statement makes explicit a position that puts forward a premise or argument to be communicated or proven. The thesis and introduction make clear what to expect from the rest of the paper and presents background information or a way to understand the subject or topic.	A general thesis statement takes a position. There is some sense as to what to expect from the rest of the paper.	There is an attempt at a thesis statement, yet the position is not clearly stated. It is not clear what to expect from the rest of the paper.	There is no statement that takes a position.
Topic Sentence and Body	A topic sentence effectively supports the thesis statement and conveys the main idea of the paragraph.	A topic sentence generally supports the thesis statement and somewhat conveys the main idea of the paragraph.	There is little sense that the topic sentence supports the thesis statement or conveys the main idea of the paragraph.	A topic sentence does not exist.
Supporting Evidence and Body	There is a complete body of evidence (facts, anecdotal story, and thought) that supports the main idea as stated in the topic sentence.	There is some evidence (facts, anecdotal story, and thought), supporting the main idea as stated in a topic sentence.	There is limited evidence (facts, anecdotal story, and thought) supporting the main idea as stated in a topic sentence.	There is no evidence (facts, anecdotal mini stories, and thought) that demonstrates the main idea.
Closing Statement	There is an effective restatement of the thesis. The closing brings a satisfactory conclusion to the position or argument. The reader is left thinking, believing in the position, and/or changes her/his thinking.	There is a general restatement of the thesis. The closing brings some conclusion to the position or argument.	There is a partial restatement of the thesis, but the closing ineffectively brings a conclusion to the position or argument.	There is no restatement of the thesis and no conclusion to the position or argument.

Volume & Clarity

Fluency, Expression, & Pace

Body Language & Eye Contact

Preparation & Rehearsal

Traits of Presentation Rubric

Traits of Presentation	4 Exemplary	3 Proficient	2 Developing	1 Beginning
Volume & Clarity	Always speaks clearly and loud enough so that the audience can hear and understand what is said.	Most often speaks clearly and loud enough so that the audience can hear and understand what is said.	Sometimes speaks clearly and loud enough so that the audience can hear and understand what is said.	Seldom speaks clearly and loud enough so that the audience can hear and understand what is said.
Fluency, Expression, & Pace	Words flow smoothly and naturally. Changes tone to match the meaning of words. Varies pace by slowing down, speeding up, and pausing for effect.	Most often words flow smoothly and naturally. Sometimes changes tone to match the meaning of words. Sometimes varies pace by slowing down, speeding up, and pausing for effect.	Occasionally words flow smoothly and naturally. Seldom changes tone to match the meaning of words. Seldom varies pace by slowing down, speeding up, and pausing for effect.	Seldom speaks fluently. Does not use expression or pace.
Body Language & Eye Contact	Uses a variety of stances. Body movement and hand gestures are used in unison with words to emphasize points or ideas. Poise demonstrates confidence and grace. Eye contact with the audience is maintained.	Most often uses a variety of stances. Most often uses body movement and hand gestures in unison with words to emphasize points or ideas. Most often makes eye contact with the audience.	Sometimes uses a variety of stances. Sometimes uses body movement and hand gestures in unison with words to emphasize points or ideas. Sometimes makes eye contact with the audience.	Seldom uses body movement or hand gestures. Seldom makes eye contact with the audience.
Preparation & Rehearsal	It is evident that thought and purpose were invested in the presentation. Materials, such as visual aids and hand-outs were gathered and organized in advance. It is evident that there has been an significant investment in rehearsal and practice.	It is somewhat evident that thought and purpose were invested in the presentation. Some materials, such as visual aids and hand-outs, were gathered and organized in advance. Some investment in rehearsal and practice is evident.	There is little evidence that thought and purpose were invested in the presentation. Limited materials were gathered or organized in advance. It seems there was a limited investment in rehearsal and practice.	It is not evident that thought and purpose were invested in the presentation. No materials were gathered and organized in advance. It seems that there was no rehearsal and practice.

Word Web Graphic Organizer

Learning the terms found in the Literacy Mats Glossary with the **word web**,
we build and shape understanding of vocabulary beyond memorizing the definitions.

(word)

(is)

(is not)

(definition in your own words)

(example)

(non-example)

(syllabication)

(dictionary definition)

(part of speech)

(word used in a sentence)

glossary

glossary
of academic vocabulary

a　**academic achievement**
the successful learning and application of knowledge, understanding, and skills within core academic subject areas such as language arts, social studies, mathematics, and science

academic standards
the common measures of what the learner is expected to understand, know, or be able to do within core academic subject areas such as language arts, social studies, mathematics, and science

active listener
a person who demonstrates the ability to listen to others' comments and ask relevant questions or build upon what they say

alliteration
a type of figurative language in which there is a repetition of sounds at the beginning of words in a phrase or sentence
Grandpa grabbed the green grapes right from the vine.

analyze
to examine and consider the constitution or structure of a thing or topic in order to discover its attributes, features, and meaning

analytical comprehension
understanding a piece of writing for its quality; to look at a piece of writing not just as a reader, but also through the eyes of a writer, in order to appreciate the writer's craft; the act of evaluating writing against the six Traits of Writing:
ideas, organization, voice, word choice, sentence fluency, and conventions

anchor
a sample of writing that is intended to model the quality of writing against the six Traits of Writing

audience
a group of people for whom a piece of writing or presentation is intended

author's purpose
what the writer intends to achieve with his or her audience

b　**background knowledge**
the knowledge and understanding one already has relative to a specific subject

glossary
of academic vocabulary

body language
the use of posture, body and hand movement, and poise to communicate

book club
a group of learners who have agreed to read a common text and then come together to engage in meaningful conversation to build and shape their literal, inferential, and analytical comprehension

brainstorm
a process by which one produces ideas or solves a problem by rapidly generating as many ideas, words, phrases, and varieties of solutions as possible

C **cadence**
the rhythmic flow of speech or writing

cause and effect
noting the relationship between actions and events — one or more being the result of another

central purpose
the primary reason a piece of writing has been written; the message that it is intended to achieve; the aim, goal, or objective made clear by the subject, main ideas, and published form

character
a person, imaginary being, or animal in a story; within a story there are main characters and there may be secondary characters

clarity
the clearness of spoken or written language; the comprehensibility of expression; the enunciation of speech

cognitive processes
fundamental critical thinking skills: connect background knowledge, generate questions, visualize, infer, perspective and empathy, cause and effect, compare and contrast, analyze and synthesize, determine importance, monitor comprehension

compare and contrast
an exercise describing the similarities and differences between two or more people, places, things, or ideas

comprehension
the ability to understand something; the knowledge gained about something

glossary
of academic vocabulary

conclude
to arrive at a logical judgment or opinion by the process of reasoning; to infer on the basis of convincing evidence, prior knowledge, and personal experience

conflict
a problem or disagreement in a story, which typically is resolved; within a story there is a main conflict and there may be secondary conflicts

conflict, types of

person against person
a character within the story faces a problem with another person — challenges with competition, ideas, interests, or desires

person against self
a character within the story faces a problem with himself or herself — an internal struggle related to choosing between right and wrong, making a difficult decision, or self-esteem

person against nature
a character within the story faces a problem as a result of the forces of nature — the natural physical world including landscapes, weather, and animals

person against time
a character within the story faces a problem with time — to meet a deadline, make a decision, or achieve a goal

person against society
a character within the story faces a problem with a group, a community, or society — issues such as norms, rules, laws, policies, or politics

person against fate
a character within the story faces a problem perceived to be his or her destiny — a force or power perceived to predetermine events or conditions in life

connections
the relationship between the information presented and ourselves, people, the world, or other texts

conventions
a trait of good writing; the mechanics of writing — the correct use of spelling, punctuation, capitalization and grammar

glossary
of academic vocabulary

d **determine importance**
the act of deciding what knowledge is most important depending upon purpose

drafting
a phase of process writing; the act of writing a draft version of a text, such as a story or report, with the intent to revise, edit, and eventually publish

draft book
a type of composition book used by writers to develop their ability to process write in a variety of genres

e **editing**
a phase of process writing; the act of proofreading a final draft to correct all errors of conventions (capitalization, punctuation, grammar, and spelling) in preparation for publication

element
a fundamental and essential part of a story (character, setting, conflict, resolution, and plot) or information text (subject, central purpose, main ideas, supporting details, and text structure)

empathy
the ability to understand someone else's feelings or problems

enumerate
to name one-by-one and specify as in a list

engage
the act of fully participating in an activity by choice, with a sense of purpose and ownership

evaluate
the act of judging the worth of something by comparing it against certain criteria or traits

event
a social gathering, activity, or happening that takes place

evidence
information that supports an inference, interpretation, or reflection; something that indicates clearly, exemplifies, or demonstrates

example
something that is representative of a group as a whole

glossary
of academic vocabulary

explanation
a statement that makes something understood by describing the relevant structure, operation, or circumstances

expository writing
an explanatory form of writing detailing or justifying information, ideas, and opinions; a written work that tells who, what, where, why, when, and how

expression
speaking and communicating with emotion and energy; the ability to express feelings and mood with tone of speech, facial expression, and body language

eye contact
a direct look to engage the audience

f   **fact**
something that is true

figurative language
an expression that uses language in a non-literal way, such as:
simile, metaphor, personification, hyperbole, and alliteration

fiction
a literary work or story whose content is produced by the imagination and is not necessarily based on fact; genres classified as fiction include realistic fiction, science fiction, historical fiction, fantasy, fairy tale, folk tale, tall tale, fable, legend, and myth

fluency
speaking or writing a language well; the ability to express oneself effortlessly by speaking smoothly, accurately, and naturally

g   **generate questions**
the act of asking open-ended questions to extend thinking or propel reading forward

genre
the classification of types of written work; all genres may be classified as either fiction or nonfiction; samples of fiction include realistic fiction, science fiction, historical fiction, and fantasy; samples of nonfiction include autobiography, biography, report, and essay.

h   **hyperbole**
a type of figurative language in which exaggeration is used for emphasis or effect;
an exaggerated comparison: The tree was so tall it touched the clouds.

glossary
of academic vocabulary

i

ideas
a trait of writing; the main message supported by details, examples, explanations, evidence, or events

independent reader
an independent reader might be considered as one who
- reads a variety of genres for purpose and meaning
- is self-motivated to read on a regular basis
- engages in sustained silent reading
- comprehends with literal, inferential, and analytical understanding
- expands vocabulary continuously
- engages in shared reading, including partner or group conversation (e.g., book club) to build and shape comprehension and deepen understanding

independent writer
an independent writer might be considered as one who
- writes a variety of genres for purpose and meaning
- is self-motivated to write on a regular basis
- process writes to publish:
  prewriting, drafting, revising, editing, and publishing
- produces quality writing per the traits of writing:
  content & ideas, organization, voice, word choice, sentence fluency, and conventions
- maintains a draft book or journal

inferential comprehension
a type of reading comprehension; the reader is able to understand what has been read implicitly and arrive at insightful interpretations based upon background knowledge or personal experience, and by reflecting upon the message of the text and big ideas

information text structures
the fundamental approaches used to communicate information within expository writing

description-explanation
a description text structure shows mental images of the particulars of a story, event, person, place, or object. An explanation text structure shows a set of facts, which clarifies the context, causes, and consequences of those facts

sequence-time
a sequence-time text structure describes or explains how things happened in chronological order, including details for who did what, where, when, why, and how

informational text structure patterns (continued)

problem-solution

a problem-solution text structure shows a problem (including why there is a problem) followed by one or more possible solutions

persuasive

a persuasive text structure states a position and shows a reason or set of reasons with the aim of persuading others that an action or idea is right or wrong; the aim is to persuade someone to change their thinking, to believe something, or do something

cause-effect

a cause-effect text structure shows the connection between what has happened and its impact or result; cause is why something happened, effect is the result

compare-contrast

a compare-contrast text structure shows how two or more things are alike and/or how they are different

inquire

the act of seeking information by asking a question

interpretation

the act of expressing what is implied based upon inferences supported by evidence and influenced by text-to-text, text-to-self, and text-to-world connections

k   **knowledge**

the state or fact of knowing; recall of specific facts and information about something; the sum or range of what has been discovered, perceived, or learned

l   **lead**

an opening sentence, paragraph, or passage designed to hook the reader; leads may be classified according to the following headings and examples:

action

Her hands trembled as she opened the letter.

where

There it was at the edge of the pond.

when

It happened on the first day of winter in 1971.

lead *(continued)*

dialogue
"Did you hear what I just heard?" asked Max as he threw another log on the fire. "I did, but I wish that I hadn't," whispered Sam.

comment
It was the most magical thing I had ever seen.

question
Why would they have done that?

list
a set of names, things, etc. written one below the other

literacy
the ability to converse, read, write, and present

literal comprehension
a type of reading comprehension; the reader is able to understand what has been read word-for-word and recall the explicit content and meaning of the text

m

main character
a person, imaginary being, or animal in a story who is perceived as a primary actor within the plot

main ideas
important knowledge and understanding that supports the subject of information

meta-cognition
awareness and reflection of one's cognitive processes — thinking about thinking

metaphor
a type of figurative language, in which a word or phrase that ordinarily designates one thing is used to designate another, thus making an implicit comparison; the act of comparing two unlike things without using the words like or as
The Internet is a highway of information.

model
something which serves as an example to be learned, imitated, or compared

modeling
the act of demonstrating knowledge, understanding, or a process, with think-aloud cognitive processes and meta-cognition, and the authentic act of doing in order to help the learner know, understand, and do the same

mood

the feeling a reader gets from a story or the feeling a writer intends to convey; types of mood include happy, peaceful, sad, and angry; purposeful details and descriptions of characters, setting, and action within a story are ways an author might convey mood

monitor comprehension

the act of thinking about understanding; the ability to be comfortable asking questions about anything not understood or knowing when understanding changes

motive

an emotion, desire, need, or impulse that incites action

n **nonfiction**

an information piece of writing; the content is produced based upon facts and is intended to convey information, to persuade, or to describe; genres classified as nonfiction include report, essay, directions, instructions, autobiography, and biography

o **organization**

a trait of writing; the order and arrangement in a story or information; a logical sequence of ideas allows the reader to make sense of the story or information

outline

a final step in the prewriting phase of process writing; logically ordered ideas — recorded as words or phrases — arranged in sequence as a guide to produce a draft

p **pace**

slowing down, speeding up, or pausing for effect when speaking or reading aloud

pagination

the system by which pages are numbered in a publication

personification

a type of figurative language, in which a thing, place, or idea is given qualities of a person or represented as possessing human form

The beauty of the painting spoke to my soul.

perspective

a way of thinking about something or seeing things that is influenced by background knowledge or personal experience

phase

a stage or part of a step-by-step process

glossary
of academic vocabulary

plot
a connected series of events in a story; within a story there is a main plot and there may be subplots; a plot line has five parts:
exposition, rising action, climax, falling action, and resolution

predict
the act of foretelling what will happen next based upon text-to-text, text-to-self, and text-to-world connections

preparation
the act of organizing everything needed for reading a story aloud or making a presentation

presentation
1. the act of presenting to inform, educate, persuade, or entertain
2. the act of considering how, when, and where a piece of written work will be published

prewriting
the first phase of process writing; a variety of planning strategies used in preparation to produce a draft

process writing
a step-by-step process used when writing a story or information; process writing has five steps: prewriting, drafting, revising, editing, and publishing

proofreading
identifying and marking errors of conventions that need to be corrected such as capitalization, punctuation, grammar and spelling; part of the edit phase of process writing

publishing
the final phase of process writing; the preparation and issuing of a text form such as a novel, magazine article, or brochure for public distribution or sale

probe
to delve into and investigate a question or comment to gain a deeper understanding

r   **recall**
to remember explicit information, facts, or details that have been read or discussed

glossary
of academic vocabulary

reflection

considering, and then communicating orally or in writing, big ideas or truths relative to what we notice and think and realize

rehearsal

the act of practicing in preparation for a presentation or performance

resolution

the solving of, or solution to, a problem or disagreement in a story; within a story the resolution is usually determined toward the end; the resolution brings a natural, thought-provoking, or surprise ending to the story

respect

a feeling of being appreciative; regard and esteem for the worth of self and others

revising

a phase of process writing; returning to a draft to improve it for ideas, organization, voice, word choice, and sentence fluency

rhythm

the natural pattern of sounds and speech in language when read or written with fluency

S **secondary character**

a person, imaginary being, or animal in a story who is perceived as a supporting character within the plot

seed idea

an idea logged in a journal to develop into a narrative or non-narrative writing

sentence fluency

a trait of writing; a variety of sentence types, beginnings, and lengths flow together; writing that is easy to read with expression and pace; the writing has rhythm and cadence

setting

the time, place, and surroundings in which the story occurs — including the past, present, and future

sequence

the order in which things happen

simile

a type of figurative language, in which two essentially unlike things are compared using the words like or as:

The yard, full of fireflies, sparkled like a thousand stars in the night.

glossary
of academic vocabulary

small moment scene
stretching a small moment in time to show, not tell the setting, action, thoughts and feelings, and dialogue

subplot
a plot secondary to the main plot in a story; typically related to the main plot and, at some point in the story, intersecting with the main plot

subject
the main topic of thought, discussion, investigation, or writing

summarize
to give only the main information and ideas, not all details or specific events

supporting details
the facts or pieces of information that contribute to a main idea; details make a piece of writing more real and interesting; details give life to a description, explain an idea, provide examples, or support an argument

synthesis
the combining of separate elements, ideas, or events to make a more complete understanding

t **text features**
organizational aids and graphics used to highlight meaning such as titles, captions, illustrations, etc.

text form
the published version of a particular genre — for example, historical fiction might be published as a novel, comic book, or poem

theme
the idea central to a story; an idea or message that an author wants to communicate in a story

topic
the narrowed idea specific to a subject of a speech, essay, or discourse

topic sentence
a sentence within a paragraph that states the main idea and tells the reader the primary focus of the paragraph or section in information writing; topic sentences support the thesis and may be classified according to the following headings and examples:

glossary
of academic vocabulary

topic sentence (continued)

topic/key detail topic sentence
Process writing has multiple steps and takes time.

occasion/position topic sentence
My dog must have a bath once every two weeks, even though she does not like water!

power topic sentence
There are three good reasons why rules are important.

compare/contrast topic sentence
Max and Sam may look identical, but they are different in many ways.

transitions
words or phrases used to strengthen the flow of one idea or event to the next in a story or information

traits of conversation
the qualities of conversation:
be respectful, be prepared, be an active listener, be clear, inquire and probe, show comprehension, check understanding, and control self

traits of presentation
the qualities of presentation:
volume and clarity; fluency, expression, and pace; body language and eye contact; preparation and rehearsal

traits of writing
the qualities that are inherent in good writing:
ideas, organization, voice, word choice, sentence fluency, and conventions

V   **visualize**
to form mental sensory and emotional images

visual literacy
the use of text features appropriate to the text form chosen for publication;
the arrangement of features such as headings, captions, illustrations, colors, spacing, and layout to match the author's purpose and the needs of the audience

glossary
of academic vocabulary

voice
a trait of writing; the writer's own words and style of writing — the unique way of expressing ideas and feelings; a sense of energy and emotion; a distinctive voice helps the reader feel that a real person is behind the words

volume
the appropriate loudness of voice

W **word choice**
a trait of writing; using precise and accurate words to express meaning; precise words help the writer to convey meaning

about the author

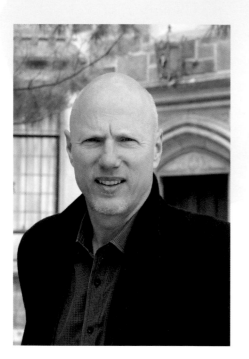

Brian Kissman

Brian Kissman has been an educator for more than 30 years. He holds a Master's Degree in Educational Leadership from Western Michigan University. He taught Elementary students for eighteen years, served as an Elementary principal for six years, and as a Director of Curriculum, Learning, and Instruction for eight years.

Over half of his career has been on the international schools circuit; in addition to being a native Michigan educator, he has lived and worked in Bali, Qatar, Hong Kong, Malaysia, Spain, Switzerland, France, Japan and Liberia West Africa.

His areas of professional interest and expertise are curriculum and instruction, literacy, purpose-designed learning environments, and professional learning communities. He has a passion for creative expression and lifelong learning.

Brian is the author of *Literacy Mats*, *Phonics Things*, and *Multiplication Mats*.